COOKING
THROUGH THE
YEAR

COOKING
THROUGH THE
YEAR

SHIRLEY GILL

Over 135 delicious seasonal dishes
Photography by Karl Adamson

SMITHMARK

This edition published in 1994
by SMITHMARK Publishers Inc.
16 East 32nd Street
New York
NY 10016
USA

SMITHMARK books are available for bulk purchase for sales and
promotion and premium use. For details write or call the manager of
special sales,
SMITHMARK Publishers Inc.
16 East 32nd Street
New York
NY 10016
(212) 532-6600

ISBN 0 8317 5655 1

Editorial Director: Joanna Lorenz
Series Editor: Linda Fraser
Designer: Tony Paine
Photographer: Karl Adamson
Food for Photography: Jane Stevenson
Props Stylist: Blake Minton

Printed and bound in Singapore

Contents

Spring

Soups, Appetizers and Snacks 8
Meat, Poultry and Game 16
Fish and Seafood 24
Vegetables, Salads and Grains 32
Desserts 38

Summer

Soups, Appetizers and Snacks 46
Meat, Poultry and Game 54
Fish and Seafood 60
Vegetables, Salads and Grains 66
Desserts 74

Autumn

Soups, Appetizers and Snacks 84
Meat, Poultry and Game 90
Fish and Seafood 98
Vegetables, Salads and Grains 106
Desserts 114

Winter

Soups, Appetizers and Snacks 122
Meat, Poultry and Game 130
Fish and Seafood 138
Vegetables, Salads and Grains 144
Desserts 150

Index 160

SPRING

Spring brings with it the first forced rhubarb, its pink tones lending so much to dishes like Rhubarb and Ginger Cheesecake, and Rhubarb Meringue Pie. Later on, gooseberries appear, sharp and full of flavor, perfect for Gooseberry and Orange Ice Cream. Now is the time for asparagus – serve it with tarragon butter, wrapped in ham and topped with Gruyère sauce, or try the very first few tender spears in a sauce with pasta. Spinach is useful in salads, as a vegetable accompaniment to fish, and in dishes such as Spinach Roulade with Mushrooms. Spring is a good time for fish – salmon, whitebait and mackerel are all at their best, and white fish are plump and plentiful. The first of the new season's lamb comes into the shops as well at this time, lean, succulent and quite delicious. Oatmeal and Herb Rack of Lamb makes a wonderful Sunday roast, and Lamb and Spring Vegetable Stew also makes the most of tender baby turnips and carrots, and young fava beans.

CARROT AND CORIANDER SOUP

Use a good homemade stock for this soup, if possible – it adds a far greater depth of flavor than stock made from cubes.

INGREDIENTS

Serves 4
4 tbsp butter
3 leeks, sliced
1lb carrots, sliced
1 tbsp ground coriander
5 cups light chicken stock
⅔ cup strained plain yogurt
salt and black pepper
2–3 tbsp chopped fresh coriander, to garnish

1 Melt the butter in a large pan. Add the leeks and carrots and stir well, coating the vegetables with the butter. Cover and cook for about 10 minutes, until the vegetables are beginning to soften but not color.

2 Stir in the ground coriander and cook for about 1 minute. Pour in the stock and add seasoning to taste. Bring to a boil, cover and simmer for about 20 minutes, until the leeks and carrots are tender.

3 Leave to cool slightly, then purée the soup in a blender until smooth. Return the soup to the pan and add 2 tbsp of the yogurt, then taste the soup and adjust the seasoning. Reheat gently but do not boil.

4 Ladle the soup into bowls and put a spoonful of the remaining yogurt in the center of each. Scatter over the coriander and serve immediately.

LEEK, POTATO AND ARUGULA SOUP

Arugula, with its distinctive, peppery taste, is wonderful in this filling and satisfying soup. Serve it hot with ciabatta croûtons.

INGREDIENTS

Serves 4–6
4 tbsp butter
1 onion, chopped
3 leeks, chopped
2 potatoes, diced
3¾ cups light chicken stock
  or water
2 large handfuls arugula, roughly
  chopped
⅔ cup heavy cream
salt and black pepper
garlic-flavored ciabatta croûtons,
  to serve

1 Melt the butter in a large heavy-based pan, add the onion, leeks and potatoes and stir until the vegetables are coated in butter.

2 Cover and leave the vegetables to sweat for about 15 minutes. Pour in the stock, cover once again, then simmer for a further 20 minutes, until the vegetables are tender.

3 Press the soup through a sieve or food mill and return to the rinsed-out pan. (When puréeing the soup, don't use a blender or food processor, as these will give the soup a gluey texture.) Add the chopped arugula and cook gently for 5 minutes.

4 Stir in the cream, then season to taste and reheat gently. Ladle the soup into warmed soup bowls, then serve with a few garlic-flavored ciabatta croûtons in each.

Hot Tomato and Mozzarella Salad

A quick, easy appetizer with a Mediterranean flavor. It can be prepared in advance, chilled, then broiled just before serving.

INGREDIENTS

Serves 4

1lb plum tomatoes, sliced
8oz mozzarella cheese, sliced
1 red onion, finely chopped
4–6 pieces sun-dried tomatoes in oil,
*   drained and chopped*
4 tbsp olive oil
1 tsp red wine vinegar
½ tsp Dijon mustard
4 tbsp chopped fresh mixed herbs,
*   such as basil, parsley, oregano*
*   and chives*
salt and black pepper
fresh herb sprigs, to garnish (optional)

1 Arrange the sliced tomatoes and mozzarella in circles in four individual shallow flameproof dishes.

2 Scatter over the chopped onion and sun-dried tomatoes.

3 Whisk together the olive oil, vinegar, mustard, chopped herbs and seasoning. Pour over the salads.

4 Place the salads under a hot broiler for 4–5 minutes, until the mozzarella starts to melt. Grind over plenty of black pepper and serve garnished with fresh herb sprigs, if liked.

Asparagus with Tarragon Butter

Eating fresh asparagus with your fingers can be messy, but, never mind, it is the only proper way to eat it!

INGREDIENTS

Serves 4

1¼lb fresh asparagus
½ cup butter
2 tbsp chopped fresh tarragon
1 tbsp chopped fresh parsley
grated rind of ½ lemon
1 tbsp lemon juice
salt and black pepper

COOK'S TIP
When buying fresh asparagus, choose spears which are plump and have a good even color with tightly budded tips.

1 Trim the woody ends from the asparagus spears, then tie them into four equal bundles.

2 Place the bundles of asparagus in a large frying pan with about 1in boiling water. Cover and cook for about 6–8 minutes, until the asparagus is tender but still firm. Drain well and discard the strings.

3 Meanwhile, melt the butter in a small pan. Add the tarragon, parsley, lemon rind and juice and seasoning.

4 Arrange the asparagus spears on four warmed serving plates. Pour the hot tarragon butter over the asparagus and serve at once.

SPINACH SALAD WITH BACON AND SHRIMP

Serve this hot salad with plenty of crusty bread for mopping up the delicious juices.

INGREDIENTS

Serves 4
7 tbsp olive oil
2 tbsp sherry vinegar
2 garlic cloves, finely chopped
1 tsp Dijon mustard
12 cooked jumbo shrimp
4oz lean bacon, rinded and cut into strips
about 4oz fresh young spinach leaves
½ head oak leaf lettuce, roughly torn
salt and black pepper

1 To make the dressing, whisk together 6 tbsp of the olive oil with the vinegar, garlic, mustard and seasoning in a small pan. Heat gently until thickened slightly, then keep warm.

2 Carefully peel the shrimp, leaving the tails intact. Set aside.

3 Heat the remaining oil in a frying pan and fry the bacon until golden and crisp, stirring occasionally. Add the shrimp and stir-fry for a few minutes until warmed through.

4 While the bacon and shrimp are cooking, arrange the spinach and torn oak leaf lettuce leaves on four individual serving plates.

5 Spoon the bacon and shrimp on to the leaves, then pour over the hot dressing. Serve at once.

COOK'S TIP
Sherry vinegar lends its pungent flavor to this delicious salad. You can buy it from larger supermarkets and gourmet stores.

SMOKED TROUT WITH CUCUMBER SALAD

Smoked trout provides an easy and delicious first course. Serve it at room temperature for the best flavor.

INGREDIENTS

Serves 4
1 large cucumber
4 tbsp crème fraîche or strained plain
   yogurt
1 tbsp chopped fresh dill
4 smoked trout fillets
salt and black pepper
dill sprigs, to garnish
crusty whole wheat bread, to serve

1 Peel the cucumber, cut in half lengthwise and scoop out the seeds using a teaspoon. Cut into tiny dice.

2 Put the cucumber in a colander set over a plate and sprinkle with salt. Leave to drain for at least 1 hour to draw out the excess moisture.

3 Rinse the cucumber well, then pat dry on paper towels. Transfer the diced cucumber to a bowl and stir in the crème fraîche or yogurt, chopped dill and some freshly ground pepper. Chill the cucumber salad for about 30 minutes.

4 Arrange the trout fillets on individual plates. Spoon the cucumber and dill salad on one side and grind over a little black pepper. Garnish with dill sprigs and serve with crusty bread.

LEEK TERRINE WITH DELI MEATS

This attractive appetizer is very simple to make yet looks spectacular. You can make the terrine a day ahead and keep it covered in the refrigerator. If your guests are vegetarian offer chunks of feta cheese.

INGREDIENTS

Serves 6
20–24 small young leeks
4 tbsp walnut oil
4 tbsp olive oil
2 tbsp white wine vinegar
1 tsp whole grain mustard
about 8oz mixed sliced meats, such as prosciutto, Genoa salami or mortadella
⅔ cup walnuts, toasted and chopped
salt and black pepper

1 Cut off the roots and most of the green part from the leeks. Wash them thoroughly under cold running water to get rid of any grit or mud.

2 Bring a large pan of salted water to a boil. Add the leeks, bring the water back to a boil, then reduce the heat and simmer for 6–8 minutes, until the leeks are just tender. Drain well.

3 Fill a 1lb loaf pan with the leeks, placing them alternately head to tail and sprinkling each layer as you go with salt and pepper.

4 Put another loaf pan inside the first and gently press down on the leeks. Carefully invert both pans and let any water drain out.

5 Place one or two weights on top of the pans and chill the terrine for at least 4 hours, or overnight.

6 Meanwhile, make the dressing. Whisk together the walnut and olive oils, vinegar and whole grain mustard in a small bowl. Add seasoning to taste.

7 Carefully turn out the terrine on to a board and cut into slices using a large sharp knife. Lay the slices of leek terrine on serving plates and arrange the slices of meat alongside.

8 Spoon the dressing over the slices of terrine and scatter over the chopped walnuts. Serve at once.

COOK'S TIP
For this terrine, it is important to use tender young leeks. The white part mainly is used in this recipe, but the green tops can be used in soups. The terrine must be pressed for at least 4 hours – this makes it easier to carve into slices. You can vary the sliced meats as you like. Try smoked beef, salami, smoked venison or baked ham.

VARIATION
If you are short of time, serve the cooked leeks simply marinated in the walnut and mustard dressing.

GINGER PORK WITH BLACK BEAN SAUCE

INGREDIENTS

Serves 4
12oz pork fillet
1 garlic clove, crushed
1 tbsp grated fresh ginger root
6 tbsp chicken stock
2 tbsp dry sherry
1 tbsp light soy sauce
1 tsp sugar
2 tsp cornstarch
3 tbsp groundnut oil
2 yellow bell peppers, seeded and cut into strips
2 red bell peppers, seeded and cut into strips
1 bunch scallions, diagonally sliced
3 tbsp preserved black beans, coarsely chopped
coriander sprigs, to garnish

1 Cut the pork into thin slices across the grain of the meat. Put the slices into a dish and mix them with the garlic and ginger. Leave to marinate at room temperature for 15 minutes.

2 Blend together the stock, sherry, soy sauce, sugar and cornstarch in a small bowl, then set the sauce mixture aside.

3 Heat the oil in a wok or large frying pan, add the marinated pork and stir-fry for 2–3 minutes. Add the peppers and scallions and stir-fry for a further 2 minutes.

4 Add the beans and sauce mixture and cook, stirring until thick. Serve hot, garnished with coriander.

ASPARAGUS AND HAM GRATIN

Choose plump green asparagus spears and the best cooked ham for this tasty gratin – it's a good way of stretching a small quantity of asparagus! Serve with warm crusty bread.

INGREDIENTS

Serves 4
12 asparagus spears
6 slices baked ham, halved
3 tbsp butter
⅓ cup flour
1⅞ cups milk
2 tsp Dijon mustard
3oz Gruyère cheese, grated
freshly grated nutmeg
1oz Parmesan cheese, finely grated
7 tbsp fresh fine white bread crumbs
salt and black pepper

1 Preheat the oven to 375°F. Trim the woody ends from the asparagus, then place the spears in a large frying pan with about 1in boiling water. Cover the pan and cook for 4 minutes, then drain thoroughly.

2 Wrap a slice of baked ham around each asparagus spear and arrange in a shallow buttered ovenproof dish.

3 Melt the butter in a pan. Add the flour and cook for 1 minute, stirring. Gradually add the milk, then bring to a boil, stirring to give a smooth sauce. Stir in the mustard, Gruyère, salt, pepper and nutmeg to taste.

4 Pour the sauce over the asparagus. Mix the Parmesan cheese with the bread crumbs and sprinkle evenly over the top. Bake for about 20 minutes, until browned on top and bubbling. Serve immediately.

OATMEAL AND HERB RACK OF LAMB

Ask the butcher to remove the chine bone for you (this is the long bone that runs along the eye of the meat) – this will make carving easier.

INGREDIENTS

Serves 6
2 best end necks of lamb, about 2lb each
finely grated rind of 1 lemon
4 tbsp medium oatmeal
1 cup fresh white bread crumbs
4 tbsp chopped fresh parsley
2 tbsp butter, melted
2 tbsp honey
salt and black pepper
roasted baby vegetables and gravy, to serve
fresh herb sprigs, to garnish

1 Preheat the oven to 400°F. Using a small sharp knife, carefully cut through the skin and meat about 1in from the tips of the bones. Pull off the fatty meat to expose the bones, then scrape around each bone tip until it is completely clean.

2 Trim all the skin and most of the fat off the meat, then lightly score the fat. Repeat with the second rack.

3 Mix together the lemon rind, oatmeal, bread crumbs, parsley and seasoning, then stir in the melted butter.

4 Brush the fatty side of each rack with honey, then press the oatmeal mixture evenly over the surface.

5 Place the racks in a roasting pan with the oatmeal sides uppermost. Roast for 40–50 minutes, depending on whether you like rare or medium lamb. Cover loosely with foil if browning too much. To serve, slice each rack into three and accompany with roasted baby vegetables and gravy made with the pan juices. Garnish with fresh herb sprigs.

SKEWERS OF LAMB WITH MINT

──── INGREDIENTS ────

Serves 4

1¼ cups strained plain yogurt
½ garlic clove, crushed
good pinch saffron powder
2 tbsp chopped fresh mint
2 tbsp honey
3 tbsp olive oil
3 lamb neck fillets, about 1½lb each
1 medium eggplant
2 small red onions, quartered
salt and black pepper
small mint leaves, to garnish
mixed salad and hot pita bread,
    to serve

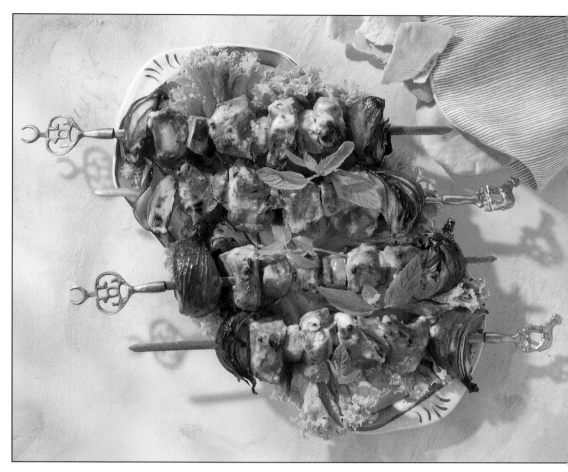

1 In a shallow dish, mix together the yogurt, garlic, saffron, mint, honey, oil and freshly ground black pepper.

2 Trim the lamb and cut into 1in cubes. Add to the marinade and stir until well coated. Cover and leave to marinate for at least 4 hours, or preferably overnight.

3 Cut the eggplant into 1in cubes and blanch in boiling salted water for 1–2 minutes. Drain well and pat dry on paper towels.

4 Remove the lamb cubes from the marinade. Thread the lamb, egg-plant and onion pieces alternately on to skewers. Broil for 10–12 minutes, turning and basting occasionally with the marinade, until the lamb is tender.

5 Serve the skewers garnished with mint leaves and accompanied by a mixed salad and hot pita bread.

COOK'S TIP
If using bamboo skewers, soak them in cold water before use to keep them from burning.

LAMB AND SPRING VEGETABLE STEW

You could also add a few blanched asparagus spears or young green beans to this version of the creamy-colored stew known as a *blanquette*.

─────── INGREDIENTS ───────

Serves 4
5 tbsp butter
2lb lean boneless shoulder of lamb,
  cut into 1½in cubes
2½ cups lamb stock or water
⅔ cup dry white wine
1 onion, quartered
2 thyme sprigs
1 bay leaf
8oz pearl onions, halved
8oz baby carrots
2 small turnips, quartered
6oz shelled fava beans
1 tbsp flour
1 egg yolk
3 tbsp heavy cream
2 tsp lemon juice
salt and black pepper
2 tbsp chopped fresh parsley,
  to garnish

1 Melt 2 tbsp of the butter in a large pan, add the lamb and sauté for about 2 minutes to seal the meat; do not allow it to color.

2 Pour in the stock or water and wine, bring to a boil, then skim the surface. Add the quartered onion, thyme and bay leaf. Cover and simmer for 1 hour.

3 Meanwhile, melt 1 tbsp of the remaining butter in a frying pan over a moderate heat, add the pearl onions and brown lightly.

4 Add the browned pearl onions, carrots and turnips to the lamb and continue to cook for 20 minutes. Add the shelled fava beans and cook for a further 10 minutes, until the vegetables and lamb are tender.

5 Lift out the lamb and vegetables from the pan and arrange in a warmed serving dish. Cover and keep warm in low oven.

6 Discard the onion quarters and herbs. Strain the stock and carefully skim off all the fat. Return the stock to the pan and boil rapidly over a high heat until the liquid has reduced to about 1⅞ cups.

7 Mix the remaining butter and the flour together to form a smooth paste. Whisk into the hot stock until thickened. Simmer for 2–3 minutes.

8 Blend together the egg yolk and cream in a bowl. Stir in a little of the hot sauce, then stir this back into the sauce. Reheat gently but do not boil. Add the lemon juice and season to taste with salt and pepper.

9 Pour the sauce over the lamb and vegetables, then sprinkle with the chopped parsley. Serve at once.

> COOK'S TIP
> The appearance of this dish improves if the tough outer skin of the shelled fava beans is removed to reveal the bright green color. Blanch the beans for 1 minute in boiling water, drain and refresh, then slit the skins and squeeze out the inner beans.

ROCK CORNISH HENS IN VERMOUTH

Serves 4
4 Rock Cornish hens, about
   1lb each
4 tbsp butter, softened
2 shallots, chopped
4 tbsp chopped fresh parsley
8oz white grapes, preferably
   muscatel, halved and seeded
⅔ cup white vermouth
1 tsp cornstarch
4 tbsp heavy cream
2 tbsp pine nuts, toasted
salt and black pepper
watercress sprigs, to garnish

1 Preheat the oven to 400°F. Wash and dry the Cornish hens. Spread the softened butter all over the birds and put a hazelnut-sized piece in the cavity of each.

2 Mix together the shallots and parsley and place a quarter of the mixture inside each bird. Put them side by side in a large roasting pan and roast for 40–50 minutes, or until the juices run clear when the thickest part of the flesh is pierced with a skewer. Transfer the Cornish hens to a warmed serving plate. Cover and keep warm.

3 Skim off most of the fat from the roasting pan, then add the grapes and vermouth. Place the pan directly over a low flame for a few minutes to warm and slightly soften the grapes.

4 Lift the grapes out of the pan using a slotted spoon and scatter them around the birds. Keep covered. Stir the cornstarch into the cream, then add to the pan juices. Cook gently for a few minutes, stirring, until the sauce has thickened. Taste and adjust seasoning.

5 Pour the sauce around the Cornish hens. Sprinkle with the toasted pine nuts and garnish with watercress sprigs.

CHICKEN PARCELS WITH HERB BUTTER

INGREDIENTS

Serves 4
4 chicken breast fillets, skinned
10 tbsp butter, softened
6 tbsp chopped fresh mixed herbs,
    such as thyme, parsley, oregano
    and rosemary
1 tsp lemon juice
5 large sheets filo pastry, defrosted
    if frozen
1 egg, beaten
2 tbsp grated Parmesan cheese
salt and black pepper

1 Season the chicken fillets and fry in 2 tbsp of the butter to seal and brown lightly. Allow to cool.

2 Preheat the oven to 375°F. Put the remaining butter, the herbs, lemon juice and seasoning in a food processor and process until smooth. Melt half the herb butter.

3 Take one sheet of filo pastry and brush with herb butter. Fold the filo pastry sheet in half and brush again with butter. Place a chicken fillet about 1in from the top end.

4 Dot the chicken with a quarter of the remaining herb butter. Fold in the sides of the pastry, then roll up to enclose it completely. Place seam-side down on a lightly greased baking sheet. Repeat with the other chicken fillets.

5 Brush the filo parcels with beaten egg. Cut the last sheet of filo into strips, then scrunch and arrange on top. Brush the parcels once again with the egg glaze, then sprinkle with Parmesan. Bake for about 35–40 minutes, until golden brown. Serve hot.

MACKEREL WITH MUSTARD AND LEMON

Mackerel must be really fresh to be enjoyed. Look for bright, firm-looking fish.

INGREDIENTS

Serves 4
4 fresh mackerel, about 10oz each, gutted and cleaned
6–8oz young spinach leaves

For the mustard and lemon butter
½ cup butter, melted
2 tbsp whole grain mustard
grated rind of 1 lemon
2 tbsp lemon juice
3 tbsp chopped fresh parsley
salt and black pepper

1 To prepare each mackerel, cut off the heads just behind the gills, using a sharp knife, then cut along the belly so that the fish can be opened out flat.

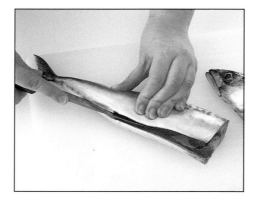

2 Place the fish on a board, skin-side up, and, with the heel of your hand, press along the backbone to loosen it.

3 Turn the fish the right way up and pull the bone away from the flesh. Remove the tail and cut each fish in half lengthwise. Wash and pat dry.

4 Score the skin three or four times, then season the fish. To make the mustard and lemon butter, mix together the melted butter, mustard, lemon rind and juice, parsley and seasoning. Place the mackerel on a broiling rack. Brush a little of the butter over the mackerel and broil for 5 minutes each side, basting occasionally, until cooked through.

5 Arrange the spinach leaves in the center of four large plates. Place the mackerel on top. Heat the remaining butter in a small pan until sizzling and pour over the mackerel. Serve at once.

WHITEBAIT WITH HERB SANDWICHES

Whitebait are the tiny fry of sprats or herring and are always served whole. Add enough cayenne pepper to make them spicy hot.

INGREDIENTS

Serves 4

unsalted butter, for spreading
6 slices whole grain bread
6 tbsp chopped fresh mixed herbs, such as parsley, chervil and chives
1lb whitebait, defrosted if frozen
5 tbsp flour
1 tbsp chopped fresh parsley
salt and cayenne pepper
groundnut oil, for deep-frying
parsley sprigs and lemon slices, to garnish

1 Butter the bread slices. Sprinkle the herbs over three of the slices, then top with the remaining slices of bread. Remove the crusts and cut each sandwich into eight triangles. Cover with plastic wrap and set aside.

2 Rinse the whitebait thoroughly. Drain and pat dry on paper towels.

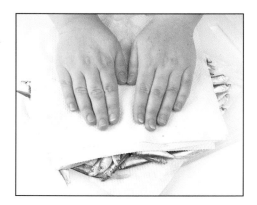

3 Put the flour, chopped parsley, salt and cayenne pepper into a large plastic bag and shake to mix. Add the whitebait and toss gently in the seasoned flour until lightly coated. Heat the oil in a deep-fat fryer to 350°F.

4 Fry the fish in batches for 2–3 minutes, until golden and crisp. Lift out of the oil and drain on paper towels. Keep warm in the oven until all the fish are cooked.

5 Sprinkle the whitebait with salt and more cayenne pepper and garnish with the parsley and lemon slices. Serve at once with the herb sandwiches.

SOLE GOUJONS WITH LIME MAYONNAISE

This simple dish can be rustled up very quickly. It makes an excellent light lunch or supper.

INGREDIENTS

Serves 4
scant 1 cup good-quality
   mayonnaise
1 small garlic clove, crushed
2 tsp capers, rinsed and chopped
2 tsp chopped gherkins
finely grated rind of ½ lime
2 tsp lime juice
1 tbsp chopped fresh coriander
1½lb sole fillets, skinned
2 eggs, beaten
2 cups fresh white bread
   crumbs
oil, for deep-frying
salt and black pepper
lime wedges, to serve

1 To make the lime mayonnaise, mix together the mayonnaise, garlic, capers, gherkins, lime rind and juice and chopped coriander. Season with salt and pepper. Transfer to a serving bowl and chill until required.

2 Cut the sole fillets into finger-length strips. Dip into the beaten egg, then into the bread crumbs.

3 Heat the oil in a deep-fat fryer to 350°F. Add the fish in batches and fry until golden brown and crisp. Drain on paper towels.

4 Pile the goujons on to warmed serving plates and serve with the lime wedges for squeezing over. Pass the sauce round separately.

SPICY FISH RÖSTI

Serve these fish cakes crisp and hot for lunch or supper with a mixed green salad.

INGREDIENTS

Serves 4
12oz large, firm waxy
   potatoes
12oz salmon or cod fillet, skinned
   and boned
3–4 scallions, finely chopped
1 tsp grated fresh ginger root
2 tbsp chopped fresh
   coriander
2 tsp lemon juice
2–3 tbsp sunflower oil
salt and cayenne pepper
lemon wedges, to serve
coriander sprigs, to garnish

1 Cook the potatoes with their skins on in a pan of boiling salted water for 10 minutes. Drain and leave to cool for a few minutes.

2 Meanwhile, finely chop the salmon or cod fillet and put into a bowl. Stir in the chopped scallions, grated ginger root, chopped coriander and lemon juice. Season to taste with salt and cayenne pepper.

3 When the potatoes are cool enough to handle, peel off the skins and grate the potatoes coarsely. Gently stir the grated potato into the fish mixture.

4 Form the fish mixture into 12 cakes, pressing the mixture together and leaving the edges slightly rough.

5 Heat the oil in a large frying pan, and, when hot, fry the fish cakes a few at a time for 3 minutes on each side, until golden brown and crisp. Drain on paper towels. Serve hot with lemon wedges for squeezing over. Garnish with sprigs of coriander.

MEDITERRANEAN FISH ROLLS

Sun-dried tomatoes, pine nuts and anchovies make a really flavorful combination for the stuffing mixture.

INGREDIENTS

Serves 4

4 sole fillets, about 8oz each, skinned
6 tbsp butter
1 small onion, chopped
1 celery stalk, finely chopped
2 cups fresh white bread crumbs
3 tbsp chopped fresh parsley
2 tbsp pine nuts, toasted
3–4 pieces sun-dried tomatoes in oil, drained and chopped
2oz can anchovy fillets, drained and chopped
5 tbsp fish stock
black pepper

1 Preheat the oven to 350°F. Using a sharp knife, carefully cut the sole fillets in half lengthwise to make eight smaller fillets.

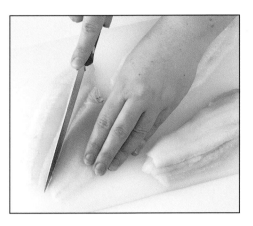

2 Melt the butter in a pan and add the onion and celery. Cover and cook over a low heat for about 15 minutes until softened. Do not allow to brown.

3 Mix together the bread crumbs, parsley, pine nuts, sun-dried tomatoes and anchovies. Stir in the softened vegetables with the buttery juices and season with pepper.

4 Divide the stuffing into eight portions. Taking one portion at a time, form the stuffing into balls, then roll up each one inside a sole fillet. Secure each roll with a toothpick.

5 Place the rolled-up fillets in a buttered ovenproof dish. Pour in the stock and cover the dish with buttered foil. Bake for about 20 minutes, or until the fish flakes easily. Remove the toothpicks, then serve with a little of the cooking juices drizzled over.

SALMON WITH WATERCRESS SAUCE

Adding the watercress right at the end of cooking retains much of its flavor and color.

INGREDIENTS

Serves 4

1¼ cups heavy cream
2 tbsp chopped fresh tarragon
2 tbsp unsalted butter
1 tbsp sunflower oil
4 salmon fillets, skinned and boned
1 garlic clove, crushed
½ cup dry white wine
1 bunch watercress
salt and black pepper

1 Gently heat the cream in a small pan until just beginning to boil. Remove the pan from the heat and stir in half the tarragon. Leave the herb cream to infuse while you cook the fish.

2 Heat the butter and oil in a frying pan, add the salmon and fry for 3–5 minutes on each side. Remove from the pan and keep warm.

3 Add the garlic and fry for 1 minute, then pour in the wine and let it bubble until reduced to about 1 tbsp.

4 Meanwhile, strip the leaves off the watercress stalks and chop finely. Discard any damaged leaves. (Save the watercress stalks for soup, if you like.)

5 Strain the herb cream into the pan and cook for a few minutes, stirring until the sauce has thickened. Stir in the remaining tarragon and watercress, then cook for a few minutes, until wilted but still bright green. Season and serve at once, spooned over the salmon.

Cod Baked with Tomato Sauce

For the best flavor, use firm ripe tomatoes for the sauce and make sure it is thick before spooning over the cod.

───── INGREDIENTS ─────

Serves 4

2 tbsp olive oil
1 onion, chopped
2 garlic cloves, finely chopped
1lb tomatoes, peeled, seeded and
   chopped
1 tsp tomato paste
4 tbsp dry white wine
4 tbsp chopped flat leaf parsley
4 cod steaks
2 tbsp dried bread crumbs
salt and black pepper
new potatoes and green salad, to serve

1 Preheat the oven to 375°F/. Heat the oil in a pan and fry the onion for about 5 minutes. Add the garlic, tomatoes, tomato paste, wine and seasoning. Bring just to a boil, then reduce the heat slightly and cook, uncovered, for about 15–20 minutes until thick. Stir in the chopped parsley.

2 Place the cod steaks in a shallow greased ovenproof dish and spoon an equal quantity of the tomato sauce on to each piece. Sprinkle the dried bread crumbs over the top.

3 Bake for 20–30 minutes, basting occasionally, until the bread crumbs are golden and crisp. Serve with new potatoes and a green salad.

Sole with Cider and Cream

───── INGREDIENTS ─────

Serves 4

4 tbsp butter
1 onion, chopped
8 lemon sole fillets, about 4oz
   each, skinned
1¼ cups cider
⅔ cup fish stock
few parsley stalks
4oz button mushrooms, sliced
4oz cooked, peeled shrimp, defrosted
   if frozen
1 tbsp each flour and butter,
   blended together to make a
   beurre manié
½ cup heavy cream
salt and black pepper
chopped fresh parsley, to garnish

1 Melt 2 tbsp of the butter in a frying pan with a lid. Add the chopped onion and fry gently, stirring occasionally, until softened.

2 Lightly season the fish, then fold each into three. Place the fish in the pan, and pour over the cider and stock. Tuck in the parsley stalks. Bring to simmering point, cover and cook for 7–10 minutes, until the fish is tender.

3 Meanwhile, melt the remaining butter and cook the mushrooms in a separate pan until tender. Transfer the fish to a warmed serving plate and scatter over the shrimp. Cover and keep warm while making the sauce.

4 Strain the fish cooking juices and return to the pan. Boil rapidly until slightly reduced. Add the beurre manié a little at a time, stirring until the sauce has thickened. Stir in the cream and seasoning to taste, then heat gently.

5 Spoon the cooked mushrooms over the fish, then pour over the cream sauce. Sprinkle with chopped fresh parsley and serve at once.

TOMATO RISOTTO

Use plum tomatoes in this dish for their fresh vibrant flavor and meaty texture.

INGREDIENTS

Serves 4
1½lb firm ripe tomatoes,
  preferably plum
4 tbsp butter
1 onion, finely chopped
about 5 cups vegetable stock
1½ cups arborio rice
14oz can cannellini beans,
  drained
2oz Parmesan cheese, finely grated
salt and black pepper
10–12 basil leaves, shredded, and
  grated Parmesan cheese, to serve

1 Halve the tomatoes and scoop out the seeds into a sieve placed over a bowl. Press the seeds with a spoon to extract all the juice. Set aside.

2 Broil the tomatoes skin-side up until the skins are blackened and blistered. Rub off the skins and dice the flesh.

3 Melt the butter in a large pan, add the onion and cook for 5 minutes until beginning to soften. Add the tomatoes, the reserved juice and seasoning, then cook, stirring occasionally, for about 10 minutes.

4 Meanwhile, bring the vegetable stock to a boil in another pan.

5 Add the rice to the tomatoes and stir to coat. Add a ladleful of the stock and stir gently until absorbed. Repeat, adding a ladleful of stock at a time, until all the stock is absorbed and the rice is tender and creamy.

6 Stir in the cannellini beans and grated Parmesan and heat through for a few minutes.

7 Just before serving the risotto, sprinkle each portion with shredded basil leaves and grated Parmesan.

BROILED POLENTA WITH PEPPERS

── INGREDIENTS ──

Serves 4

scant 1 cup polenta
2 tbsp butter
1–2 tbsp chopped mixed herbs,
*   such as parsley, thyme and*
*   sage*
melted butter, for brushing
4 tbsp olive oil
1–2 garlic cloves, cut into slivers
2 roasted red bell peppers, peeled,
*   seeded and cut into strips*
2 roasted yellow bell peppers, peeled,
*   seeded and cut into strips*
1 tbsp balsamic vinegar
salt and black pepper
fresh herb sprigs, to garnish

1 Bring 2½ cups salted water to a boil in a heavy pan. Trickle in the polenta, beating continuously, then cook gently for 15–20 minutes, stirring occasionally, until the mixture is no longer grainy and comes away from the sides of the pan.

2 Remove the pan from the heat and beat in the butter, herbs and plenty of freshly ground black pepper.

3 Pour the polenta into a small deep bowl, smooth the surface and leave until cold and firm.

4 Turn out the polenta on to a board and cut into thick slices. Brush the polenta slices with melted butter and grill each side for about 4–5 minutes, until golden brown.

5 Meanwhile, heat the olive oil in a frying pan, add the garlic and peppers and stir-fry for 1–2 minutes. Stir in the balsamic vinegar and seasoning.

6 Spoon the pepper mixture over the polenta slices and garnish with fresh herb sprigs. Serve hot.

CREAMY POTATO GRATIN WITH HERBS

INGREDIENTS

Serves 4

1½lb waxy potatoes
2 tbsp butter
1 onion, finely chopped
1 garlic clove, crushed
2 eggs
1¼ cups crème fraîche or heavy
*   cream*
4oz Gruyère cheese, grated
4 tbsp chopped fresh mixed herbs,
*   such as chervil, thyme, chives*
*   and parsley*
freshly grated nutmeg
salt and black pepper

1 Place a baking sheet in the oven and preheat to 375°F.

2 Peel the potatoes and cut into matchsticks. Set aside. Melt the butter in a pan and fry the onion and garlic until softened. In a large bowl whisk together the eggs, crème fraîche or cream and half of the cheese.

3 Stir in the onion mixture, herbs, potatoes, salt, pepper and nutmeg. Spoon into a buttered ovenproof dish and sprinkle over the remaining cheese. Bake on the hot baking sheet for 50–60 minutes, until golden brown.

SPINACH ROULADE WITH MUSHROOMS

INGREDIENTS

Serves 6–8

1lb fresh spinach
1 tbsp butter
4 eggs, separated
freshly grated nutmeg
2oz Cheddar cheese, grated
salt and black pepper

For the filling
2 tbsp butter
12oz button mushrooms, chopped
4 tbsp flour
⅔ cup milk
3 tbsp heavy cream
2 tbsp snipped fresh chives

1 Preheat the oven to 375°F. Line a 9 x 13in jelly roll pan with wax paper. Wash the spinach and remove the stalks, then cook the wet leaves in a covered pan without extra water until just tender. Drain the spinach well, squeeze out all the excess moisture and then chop finely.

2 Tip the spinach into a bowl, beat in the butter and egg yolks and season with salt, pepper and nutmeg. Whisk the egg whites until stiff and fold into the spinach mixture. Spread into the pan and sprinkle with half the cheese. Bake for 10–12 minutes, until just firm.

3 Meanwhile, make the filling. Melt the butter in a pan and fry the mushrooms until tender, stir in the flour and cook for 1 minute. Gradually add the milk, then bring to a boil, stirring until thickened. Simmer for a further 2–3 minutes. Remove from the heat and stir in the cream and chives.

4 Remove the cooked roulade from the oven and turn out on to a sheet of wax paper. Peel off the lining paper and spread the roulade evenly with the mushroom filling.

5 Roll up the roulade fairly tightly and transfer to an ovenproof dish. Sprinkle over the remaining cheese and return the roulade to the oven for about 4–5 minutes to melt the cheese. Serve at once, cut into slices.

PARCELS OF BAKED BABY VEGETABLES

If baby vegetables are unavailable use larger vegetables cut into bite-sized pieces.

INGREDIENTS

Serves 2
4 tbsp unsalted butter
2 tbsp chopped fresh mixed herbs
1 garlic clove
½ tsp grated lemon rind
2 tbsp olive oil
12oz–1lb mixed baby vegetables,
  such as carrots, turnips, parsnips,
  fennel and patty-pan squash
6 pearl onions, peeled
lemon juice (optional)
salt and black pepper
shavings of Pecorino or Parmesan
  cheese or soft goat cheese, and
  crusty bread, to serve

1 Preheat the oven to 425°F. Put the butter, herbs, garlic and lemon rind in a food processor and process until blended. Season to taste.

2 Heat the oil in a frying pan or wok and stir-fry the vegetables for about 3 minutes, until lightly browned.

3 Divide the vegetables equally between two sheets of foil and dot with the herb butter. Close the parcels tightly and place on a baking sheet. Bake for 30–40 minutes, until just tender.

4 Carefully unwrap the parcels and add a squeeze of lemon juice, if needed, to perk up the flavors.

5 Serve the vegetables in the parcels or transfer to warmed soup plates. Spoon over the juices and accompany with the cheese and crusty bread.

PASTA WITH SPRING VEGETABLES

INGREDIENTS

Serves 4

4oz broccoli florets
4oz baby leeks
8oz asparagus
1 small fennel bulb
4oz fresh or frozen peas
3 tbsp butter
1 shallot, chopped
3 tbsp chopped fresh mixed herbs,
  such as parsley, thyme
  and sage
1¼ cups heavy cream
12oz dried penne pasta
salt and black pepper
freshly grated Parmesan cheese, to serve

1 Divide the broccoli florets into tiny sprigs. Cut the leeks and asparagus diagonally into 2in lengths. Trim the fennel bulb and remove any tough outer leaves. Cut into wedges, leaving the layers attached at the root ends so the pieces stay intact.

2 Cook each vegetable separately in boiling salted water until just tender – use the same water for each vegetable. Drain well and keep warm.

3 Melt the butter in a separate pan, add the chopped shallot and cook, stirring occasionally, until softened, but not browned. Stir in the herbs and cream and cook for a few minutes, until slightly thickened.

4 Meanwhile, cook the pasta in boiling salted water for 10 minutes until *al dente*. Drain well and add to the sauce with the vegetables. Toss gently and season with plenty of pepper.

5 Serve the pasta hot with a sprinkling of freshly grated Parmesan.

FRUITY RICOTTA CREAMS

Ricotta is an Italian soft cheese with a smooth texture and a mild, slightly sweet flavor. Served here with candied fruit peel and delicious semisweet chocolate, it is quite irresistible.

— INGREDIENTS —

Serves 4

1½ cups ricotta

2–3 tbsp Cointreau or other orange liqueur

2 tsp grated lemon rind

2 tbsp confectioners' sugar

⅔ cup heavy cream

5oz candied peel, such as orange, lemon and citron, finely chopped

2oz semisweet chocolate, finely chopped

chocolate curls, to decorate

amaretti biscuits, to serve (optional)

1 Using the back of a wooden spoon, push the ricotta through a fine strainer into a large bowl.

2 Add the liqueur, lemon rind and sugar to the ricotta and beat well until the mixture is light and smooth.

3 Whip the cream in a large bowl until it forms soft peaks.

4 Gently fold the cream into the ricotta mixture with the candied peel and chopped chocolate.

5 Spoon the mixture into four glass serving dishes and chill for about 1 hour. Decorate the ricotta creams with chocolate curls and serve with amaretti biscuits, if you like.

HOT FRUIT WITH MAPLE BUTTER

— INGREDIENTS —

Serves 4

1 large mango

1 large papaya

1 small pineapple

2 bananas

½ cup unsalted butter

4 tbsp pure maple syrup

ground cinnamon, for sprinkling

1 Peel the mango and cut the flesh into large pieces. Halve the papaya and scoop out the seeds. Cut into thick slices, then peel away the skin.

2 Peel and core the pineapple and slice into thin wedges. Peel the bananas then halve them lengthwise.

3 Cut the butter into small dice and place in a food processor with the maple syrup, then process until the mixture is smooth and creamy.

4 Place the mango, papaya, pineapple and banana on a broiling rack and brush with the maple syrup butter.

5 Cook the fruit under a medium heat for about 10 minutes, until just tender, turning the fruit occasionally and brushing it with the butter.

6 Arrange the fruit on a warmed serving platter and dot with the remaining butter. Sprinkle over a little ground cinnamon and serve the fruit piping hot.

COOK'S TIP
Prepare the fruit just before broiling so it won't discolor. Check the label when buying maple syrup to make sure that it is 100% pure as imitations have little of the taste of the real thing.

Rhubarb and Ginger Cheesecake

Fresh rhubarb and ginger are natural partners in this quite heavenly cheesecake.

Ingredients

Serves 6

6 tbsp butter
6oz ginger snaps, crushed
½ cup pecans, chopped
12oz rhubarb, chopped
6 tbsp sugar
2 tsp ginger syrup
3 eggs, beaten
8oz cottage cheese
2 tsp powdered gelatin
⅔ cup heavy cream, plus extra
   whipped cream, to serve

1 Lightly grease an 8in round loose-bottomed cake pan.

2 Melt the butter in a small pan and stir in the crushed ginger snaps and pecans. Press the mixture firmly into the base of the pan using a potato masher.

3 Put the rhubarb, sugar and ginger syrup into a pan, cover and cook very gently until soft. Purée in a blender or food processor until smooth.

4 Return the mixture to the pan and beat in the eggs. Cook over a low heat, stirring until the mixture thickens; do not allow it to boil or it will curdle. Remove the pan from the heat and beat in the cheese. Leave to cool.

5 Sprinkle the powdered gelatin over 2 tbsp cold water and leave to soften for a few minutes. Place the bowl over a pan of simmering water and stir until the gelatin dissolves and the liquid is clear. Cool slightly, then stir into the rhubarb mixture.

6 Whip the cream until it forms soft peaks, then fold into the rhubarb mixture. Pour into the prepared pan and chill until set. Cut into wedges and serve with extra cream.

RHUBARB MERINGUE PIE

Serves 6
1¾ cups flour
⅓ cup ground walnuts
½ cup butter, diced
generous 1½ cups sugar
4 egg yolks
1½lb rhubarb, cut into small pieces
finely grated rind and juice of 3
   blood or navel oranges
5 tbsp cornstarch
3 egg whites
whipped cream, to serve

1 Sift the flour into a bowl and add the ground walnuts. Rub in the butter until the mixture resembles fine bread crumbs. Stir in 2 tbsp of the sugar with 1 egg yolk lightly beaten with 1 tbsp water. Mix to a dough. Turn out on to a floured surface and knead lightly. Place in a plastic bag and chill for at least 30 minutes.

2 Preheat the oven to 375°F. Roll out the pastry on a lightly floured surface and use to line a 9in fluted quiche pan. Prick the base all over with a fork. Line with wax paper and fill with baking beans, then bake the crust for 15 minutes.

3 Meanwhile, put the rhubarb, 6 tbsp of the remaining sugar and the orange rind in a pan. Cover and cook gently, over a fairly low heat, until the rhubarb is tender.

4 Remove the beans and paper, then brush all over with a little of the remaining egg yolks. Bake for a further 10–15 minutes, until the pastry is crisp.

5 Blend the cornstarch with the orange juice. Off the heat, stir the cornstarch mixture into the rhubarb, then bring to a boil, stirring constantly until thickened. Cook for 1–2 minutes. Cool slightly, then beat in the remaining egg yolks. Pour into the pie crust.

6 Whisk the egg whites until they form soft peaks, then whisk in the remaining sugar, 1 tbsp at a time, whisking well after each addition.

7 Swirl the meringue over the filling to cover completely. Bake for about 25 minutes until golden, then leave to cool for about 30 minutes before serving with whipped cream.

HOT MOCHA SOUFFLÉS

These hot, sweet soufflés are easy to make, but don't be tempted to open the oven door during cooking!

─── INGREDIENTS ───

Serves 4
4 tbsp butter
⅓ cup flour
1¼ cups milk
4oz semisweet chocolate, finely chopped
1 tbsp instant coffee granules
6 tbsp sugar, plus extra for coating the dishes
5 eggs, separated
confectioners' sugar, for dusting

1 Preheat the oven to 375°F, then butter four ½ pint / 1¼ cup soufflé dishes generously, especially around the rim areas.

2 Sprinkle the dishes heavily with sugar and set aside. Melt the butter in a heavy-based pan. Stir in the flour and cook for 1 minute. Gradually add the milk and cook, stirring until thickened. Cook for 1–2 minutes, stirring.

3 Remove the pan from the heat and beat in the chopped chocolate and the coffee granules.

4 Cool the chocolate mixture slightly, then beat in the sugar and egg yolks. Whisk the egg whites until stiff but not dry. Add a spoonful to the chocolate sauce and beat in to lighten the mixture. Gently fold in the remainder.

5 Spoon the mixture into the dishes and bake for 20 minutes, or until well risen and just firm to the touch. Dust with confectioners' sugar and serve.

GOOSEBERRY AND ORANGE ICE CREAM

There is no need to stir this ice cream during freezing – it freezes to a perfect consistency.

─── INGREDIENTS ───

Serves 6
1lb gooseberries, topped and tailed
pared rind of ½ orange
4 tbsp orange juice
generous 1 cup confectioners' sugar, sifted, plus 3 tbsp
1¼ cups heavy cream
2 egg whites
candied orange peel, to decorate

1 Put the gooseberries in a pan with the orange rind and juice and the 3 tbsp confectioners' sugar. Cover the pan and cook over a low heat until the gooseberries are tender. Discard the orange rind, then press the fruit through a nylon strainer into a bowl to form a seedless purée. Leave until completely cold.

2 Whip the cream in a bowl until it forms soft peaks, then gently fold in the gooseberry purée. Set aside.

3 Place the egg whites and the remaining confectioners' sugar in a large bowl set over a pan of simmering water and whisk until the mixture is very thick and glossy. Remove the bowl from the heat and continue whisking until the mixture is cold.

4 Carefully fold the gooseberry cream into the meringue mixture. Pour into a shallow freezerproof container and freeze for several hours, until firm.

5 Leave the ice cream to soften at room temperature for about 15 minutes, then scoop into serving dishes and decorate with the candied orange peel. Serve at once.

SUMMER

This is the season for salads and light summer recipes. Herbs are flourishing and should be used liberally for their flavor and color in dishes like Marinated Goat Cheese with Herbs, and Sautéed Salmon with Cucumber. New potatoes, fresh peas, zucchini, beans, tomatoes, watercress and many varieties of lettuce are plentiful. The soft fruit season is at its peak – cherries, raspberries, strawberries, and red and black currants are readily available and superb in a host of recipes. Summertime is picnic time and many of the dishes can be easily transported. Golden Parmesan Chicken, Potato and Red Pepper Frittata, and Feta Tabbouleh in Radicchio Cups are great picnic fare. Barbecuing is fun in the summer, too. Spiced Eggplant with Mint Yogurt is easy and makes an unusual starter or side dish, while Butterflied Cumin and Garlic Lamb, Char-Broiled Squid, and Monkfish Brochettes can be left to marinate and are delicious cooked over charcoal on hot summer evenings.

TOMATO AND BASIL SOUP

In summer, when tomatoes are plentiful and cheap to buy, this is a lovely soup to make.

INGREDIENTS

Serves 4

2 tbsp olive oil
1 onion, chopped
½ tsp sugar
1 carrot, finely chopped
1 potato, finely chopped
1 garlic clove, crushed
1½lb ripe tomatoes, roughly chopped
1 tsp tomato paste
1 bay leaf
1 thyme sprig
1 oregano sprig
4 basil leaves, roughly torn
1¼ cups light chicken or vegetable
  stock
2–3 pieces sun-dried tomatoes in oil
2 tbsp shredded basil leaves
salt and black pepper

1 Heat the oil in a large pan, add the onion and sprinkle with the sugar. Cook gently for 5 minutes.

2 Add the chopped carrot and potato, cover the pan and cook over a low heat for a further 10 minutes, without browning the vegetables.

3 Stir in the garlic, tomatoes, tomato paste, herbs, stock and seasoning. Cover and cook gently for 25–30 minutes, until the vegetables are tender.

4 Remove the pan from the heat and press the soup through a sieve or food mill to extract all the skins and seeds. Taste and adjust seasoning.

5 Reheat the soup gently, then ladle into four warmed soup bowls. Finely chop the sun-dried tomatoes and mix with a little oil from the jar. Add a spoonful to each serving, then scatter the shredded basil over the top.

BAKED EGGS WITH TARRAGON

Traditional *cocotte* dishes or small ramekins can be used for this recipe, as either will take one egg perfectly.

--- INGREDIENTS ---

Serves 4
3 tbsp butter
½ cup heavy cream
1–2 tbsp chopped fresh
  tarragon
4 eggs
salt and black pepper
fresh tarragon sprigs, to garnish

1 Preheat the oven to 350°F. Lightly butter four small ovenproof dishes, then warm them up in the oven for a few minutes.

2 Meanwhile, gently warm the cream. Sprinkle some tarragon into each dish, then spoon in a little of the cream.

3 Carefully break an egg into each of the prepared ovenproof dishes, season the eggs with salt and pepper and spoon a little more of the cream over each of the eggs.

4 Add a knob of butter to each dish and place them in a roasting pan containing sufficient water to come halfway up the sides of the dishes. Bake for 8–10 minutes, until the whites are just set and the yolks still soft. Serve hot, garnished with tarragon sprigs.

MINTED MELON SALAD

This appetizer is nicest made with two different kinds of melon; choose from an orange-fleshed Cantaloupe, a pale green Crenshaw, or a sweet white-fleshed Honeydew.

——— INGREDIENTS ———

Serves 4
2 ripe melons

For the dressing
2 tbsp roughly chopped fresh mint
1 tsp sugar
2 tbsp raspberry vinegar
6 tbsp extra virgin olive oil
salt and black pepper
mint sprigs, to decorate

1 Halve the melons, then scoop out the seeds using a dessert spoon. Cut the melons into thin wedges using a large sharp knife and remove the skins.

2 Arrange the two different varieties of melon wedges alternately on four individual serving plates.

3 To make the dressing, whisk together the mint, sugar, vinegar, oil and seasoning in a small bowl, or put in a screw-top jar and shake until blended.

4 Spoon the mint dressing over the melon wedges and decorate with mint sprigs. Serve very lightly chilled.

MARINATED GOAT CHEESE WITH HERBS

These little cheeses are delicious spread on toasted slices of French bread, brushed with olive oil and rubbed with garlic.

——— INGREDIENTS ———

Serves 4–8
4 fresh soft goat cheeses
6 tbsp chopped fresh mixed parsley, thyme and oregano
2 garlic cloves, chopped
12 black peppercorns, lightly crushed
⅔ cup extra virgin olive oil
salad leaves such as green leaf or oak leaf lettuce, to serve

COOK'S TIP
Any herbs can be added to the marinade – try chervil, tarragon, chives and basil. If you prefer, reserve the herb-flavored oil, and use it to make a salad dressing.

1 Arrange the fresh goat cheeses in a single layer in a large shallow non-metallic dish.

2 Put the chopped herbs, garlic and crushed peppercorns in a blender or food processor. Start the machine, then pour in the oil and process until the mixture is fairly smooth.

3 Spoon the herb mixture over the cheeses, then cover and leave to marinate in the fridge for 24 hours, basting the cheeses occasionally.

4 Remove the cheeses from the fridge about 30 minutes before serving and allow them to come back to room temperature. Serve the cheeses on a bed of salad leaves and spoon over a little of the olive oil and herb mixture.

CRAB AND RICOTTA TARTLETS

Use the meat from a freshly cooked crab, weighing about 1 lb, if you can. Otherwise, you can use fresh or frozen crabmeat instead.

─────── INGREDIENTS ───────

Serves 4

2 cups flour
pinch of salt
½ cup butter, diced
1 cup ricotta
1 tbsp grated onion
2 tbsp freshly grated Parmesan
  cheese
½ tsp mustard powder
2 eggs, plus 1 egg yolk
8oz crabmeat
2 tbsp chopped fresh parsley
½–1 tsp anchovy paste
1–2 tsp lemon juice
salt and cayenne pepper
salad leaves, to garnish

1 Preheat the oven to 400°F. Sift the flour and salt into a bowl, add the butter and rub it in until the mixture resembles fine bread crumbs. Stir in approximately 4 tbsp cold water to make a firm dough.

2 Turn the dough on to a floured surface and knead lightly. Roll out the pastry and use to line four 4in tartlet pans. Prick the bases with a fork, then chill for 30 minutes.

3 Line the pastry cases with wax paper and fill with baking beans. Bake for 10 minutes, then remove the paper and beans. Return to the oven and bake for a further 10 minutes.

4 Place the ricotta, grated onion, Parmesan and mustard powder in a bowl and beat until soft. Gradually beat in the eggs and egg yolk.

5 Gently stir in the crabmeat and chopped parsley, then add the anchovy paste, lemon juice, salt and cayenne pepper, to taste.

6 Remove the tartlet cases from the oven and reduce the temperature to 350°F. Spoon the filling into the cases and bake for 20 minutes, until set and golden brown. Serve hot with a garnish of salad leaves.

SPICED EGGPLANT WITH MINT YOGURT

INGREDIENTS

Serves 4
2–3 eggplants
2–3 tbsp olive oil
1 tsp ground cumin
1 tsp ground coriander
¼ tsp chili powder
⅔ cup strained plain yogurt
1 garlic clove, crushed
2 tbsp chopped fresh mint, plus extra,
  to garnish
salt and black pepper

1 Slice the eggplants thickly and place in a shallow dish. Sprinkle with salt and leave to drain for 30 minutes. Rinse the eggplant slices and pat dry thoroughly with paper towels.

2 Arrange the eggplants on a baking sheet and brush with oil. Sprinkle over half of each spice. Cook under a hot broiler until softened and browned.

3 Turn over the eggplant slices, brush again with oil and sprinkle with the remaining spices. Broil for a further 4–5 minutes, until the second sides are nicely browned.

4 Meanwhile, make the mint yogurt. Mix together the yogurt, crushed garlic, mint and season to taste with plenty of freshly ground black pepper. Spoon into a small serving bowl.

5 Arrange the broiled eggplants on a serving plate, sprinkle with mint and serve with the mint yogurt.

COOK'S TIP
Salting the eggplant slices helps to extract the bitter juices.

FETA TABBOULEH IN RADICCHIO CUPS

The radicchio cups are simply a presentation idea. If you prefer, spoon the bulgur wheat mixture on to a serving plate lined with Romaine lettuce leaves.

INGREDIENTS

Serves 4

generous ⅓ cup bulgur wheat
4 tbsp olive oil
juice of 1 lemon, or more to taste
4 scallions, chopped
6 tbsp chopped flat leaf parsley
3 tbsp chopped fresh mint
2 tomatoes, peeled, seeded and diced
6oz feta cheese, cubed
salt and black pepper
1 head radicchio
flat leaf parsley sprigs, to garnish

1 Soak the bulgur wheat in cold water for 1 hour. Drain thoroughly in a sieve and press out the excess water.

2 Mix together the oil, lemon juice and seasoning in a bowl. Add the bulgur wheat, then mix well, making sure all the grains are coated with the dressing. Leave at room temperature for about 15 minutes so the bulgur wheat can absorb some of the flavors.

3 Stir in the scallions, parsley, mint, tomatoes and feta. Taste and adjust the seasoning, adding more lemon juice to sharpen the flavor, if necessary.

4 Separate out the leaves from the radicchio and select the best cup-shaped ones. Spoon a little of the tabbouleh into each one. Arrange on individual plates or on a serving platter and garnish with flat leaf parsley sprigs.

BRESAOLA, ONION AND ARUGULA SALAD

INGREDIENTS

Serves 4

2 medium onions, peeled
5–6 tbsp olive oil
juice of 1 lemon
12 thin slices bresaola
2–3oz arugula
salt and black pepper

1 Slice each onion into eight wedges through the root.

2 Arrange the onion wedges in a single layer on a broiling rack or in a flameproof dish. Brush them with a little of the olive oil and season well with salt and pepper to taste.

3 Place the onion wedges under a hot broiler and cook for about 8–10 minutes, turning once, until they are just beginning to soften and turn golden brown at the edges.

4 Meanwhile, to make the dressing, mix together the lemon juice and 4 tbsp of the olive oil in a small bowl. Add salt and black pepper to taste and whisk well until the dressing is thoroughly blended.

5 If you have broiled the onions on a broiling rack, transfer them to a shallow dish once they are cooked.

6 Pour the lemon dressing over the hot onions and leave until cold.

7 When the onions are cold, arrange the bresaola slices on individual serving plates with the onions and arugula. Spoon over any remaining dressing and serve at once.

PORK WITH MOZZARELLA AND SAGE

Here is a variation of a famous Italian dish *Saltimbocca alla Romana* – the mozzarella adds a delicious creamy flavor.

───── INGREDIENTS ─────

Serves 2–3
8oz pork tenderloin
1 garlic clove, crushed
3oz mozzarella cheese, cut into
  6 slices
6 slices prosciutto
6 large sage leaves
2 tbsp unsalted butter
salt and black pepper
potato wedges roasted in olive oil, and
  green beans, to serve

1 Trim any excess fat from the pork, then cut the pork crosswise into six pieces about 1in thick.

2 Stand each piece of tenderloin on end and bat down with a rolling pin to flatten. Rub with garlic and set aside for 30 minutes in a cool place.

3 Place a slice of mozzarella on top of each pork steak and season with salt and pepper. Lay a slice of prosciutto on top of each, crinkling it a little to fit.

4 Press a sage leaf on to each and secure with a toothpick. Melt the butter in a large heavy-based frying pan. Add the pork and cook for about 2 minutes on each side until you see the mozzarella melting. Remove the toothpicks and serve immediately with the potatoes and green beans.

REDCURRANT-GLAZED LAMB CUTLETS

Loin chops could be used instead of the rib chops to make this dish more economical.

───── INGREDIENTS ─────

Serves 4
8 lamb rib chops, about 1in thick
2 tbsp olive oil
2 tbsp red wine
½ garlic clove, chopped
4 tbsp red currant jelly
grated rind of 1 orange
2 tbsp chopped fresh mint
black pepper

1 Place the lamb chops in a shallow dish. To make the marinade, mix together the olive oil, red wine and garlic in a bowl, then season to taste with plenty of black pepper.

2 Pour the marinade over the meat, and leave to marinate for 1 hour.

3 Put the red currant jelly and orange rind in a small pan and stir over a low heat until the jelly melts. Remove from the heat and stir in the mint.

4 Lift the lamb chops from the marinade and arrange on a broiling rack. Broil or barbecue for 10–15 minutes, according to whether you like your lamb rare or medium cooked, turning occasionally and brushing frequently with the red currant glaze.

BUTTERFLIED CUMIN AND GARLIC LAMB

Ground cumin and garlic give the lamb a wonderful Middle-Eastern flavor, although you may prefer a simple oil, lemon and herb marinade instead.

INGREDIENTS

Serves 6
4lb leg of lamb
4 tbsp olive oil
2 tbsp ground cumin
4–6 garlic cloves, crushed
salt and black pepper
toasted almond and raisin-studded
  rice, to serve
coriander sprigs and lemon wedges,
  to garnish

1 To butterfly the lamb, cut away the meat from the bone using a small sharp knife. Remove any excess fat and the thin, parchment-like membrane. Bat out the meat to an even thickness, then prick the fleshy side of the lamb well with the tip of a knife.

2 In a bowl, mix together the oil, cumin and garlic and season with pepper. Spoon the mixture all over the lamb, then rub it well into the crevices. Cover and leave to marinate overnight.

3 Preheat the oven to 400°F. Spread the lamb, skin-side down, on a rack in a roasting pan. Season with salt and roast for 45–60 minutes, until crusty brown on the outside but still pink in the center.

4 Remove the lamb from the oven and leave it to rest for about 10 minutes. Cut into diagonal slices and serve with the toasted almond and raisin-studded rice. Garnish with coriander sprigs and lemon wedges.

COOK'S TIP
The lamb may be barbecued rather than broiled. Thread it on to two long skewers and set it on the grill. Barbecue for 20–25 minutes on each side, until it is cooked to your liking.

GOLDEN PARMESAN CHICKEN

Served cold with the garlicky mayonnaise these morsels of chicken make good picnic food.

INGREDIENTS

Serves 4

4 chicken breast fillets, skinned
1½ cups fresh white bread crumbs
1½oz Parmesan cheese, finely grated
2 tbsp chopped fresh parsley
2 eggs, beaten
½ cup good-quality mayonnaise
½ cup ricotta
1–2 garlic cloves, crushed
4 tbsp butter, melted
salt and black pepper

1 Cut each chicken fillet into four or five large chunks. Mix together the bread crumbs, Parmesan, parsley and seasoning in a shallow dish.

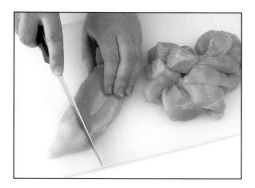

2 Dip the chicken pieces in the egg, then into the bread crumb mixture. Place in a single layer on a baking sheet and chill for at least 30 minutes.

3 Meanwhile, to make the garlic mayonnaise, mix together the mayonnaise, ricotta, garlic and pepper to taste. Spoon the mayonnaise into a small serving bowl. Chill until required.

4 Preheat the oven to 350°F. Drizzle the melted butter over the chicken pieces and cook for about 20 minutes, until they are crisp and golden. Serve the chicken immediately accompanied by a crisp green salad and the garlic mayonnaise for dipping.

DUCK, AVOCADO AND RASPBERRY SALAD

Rich duck breasts are roasted until crisp with a honey and soy glaze to serve warm with fresh raspberries and avocado. A delicious raspberry and red currant dressing adds a wonderful sweet and sour flavor.

─── INGREDIENTS ───

Serves 4

4 small or 2 large duck breasts, halved
   if large
1 tbsp honey
1 tbsp dark soy sauce
4 tbsp olive oil
1 tbsp raspberry vinegar
1 tbsp red currant jelly
selection of salad leaves, such as lamb's
   lettuce, red chicory and frisée
2 avocados, pitted, peeled and cut
   into chunks
4oz raspberries
salt and black pepper

1 Preheat the oven to 425°F. Prick the skin of each duck breast with a fork. Blend the honey and soy sauce together in a small bowl, then brush the mixture all over the skin.

2 Place the duck breasts on a rack set over a roasting pan and season with salt and pepper. Roast in the oven for 15–20 minutes, until the skins are crisp and the meat is cooked.

3 Meanwhile, to make the dressing, put the oil, vinegar, red currant jelly and seasoning in a small bowl and whisk well until evenly blended.

4 Slice the duck breasts diagonally and arrange on individual plates with the salad leaves, avocados and raspberries. Spoon over the dressing and serve immediately.

GLAZED CHINESE-STYLE SPARE RIBS

─── INGREDIENTS ───

Serves 4

4 tbsp each hoisin and soy sauce
2 tbsp honey
1 tbsp tomato paste
1 tbsp cider vinegar
2 tbsp sesame oil
¼ tsp five-spice powder
3lb pork spare ribs

1 To make the marinade, mix together all the ingredients except the ribs.

2 Place the pork ribs in a shallow non-metallic dish, large enough to take them in a single layer. Pour the marinade over the ribs, cover and leave for 4 hours, or preferably overnight, turning them occasionally.

3 Preheat the oven to 425°F. Line two large roasting pans with foil and lay the ribs in them.

4 Cook the ribs for 45 minutes (switch the pans round halfway through cooking), turning the ribs from time to time and basting them with the marinade until crisp and brown.

5 To serve, pile the ribs on to a warmed serving platter and serve hot. As the ribs are held in the fingers to eat, have large napkins at the ready.

COOK'S TIP
These ribs can also be barbecued: cook them in the oven for 30 minutes, then finish off over hot charcoal. Use a double-sided hinged wire grill, as this makes turning the ribs much easier.

WARM SALMON SALAD

Light and fresh, this salad is perfect at this time of year. Serve it immediately, or you'll find the salad leaves will lose their bright color and texture.

INGREDIENTS

Serves 4

1lb salmon fillet, skinned
2 tbsp sesame oil
grated rind of ½ orange
juice of 1 orange
1 tsp Dijon mustard
1 tbsp chopped fresh tarragon
3 tbsp groundnut oil
4oz fine green beans, trimmed
6oz mixed salad leaves, such as young
  spinach leaves, radicchio, frisée
  and oak leaf lettuce leaves
1 tbsp toasted sesame seeds
salt and black pepper

1 Cut the salmon into bite-sized pieces, then make the dressing. Mix together the sesame oil, orange rind and juice, mustard, chopped tarragon and seasoning in a bowl. Set aside.

2 Heat the groundnut oil in a frying pan. Add the salmon pieces and fry for 3–4 minutes, until lightly browned but still tender inside.

3 While the salmon is cooking, blanch the green beans in boiling salted water for about 5–6 minutes, until tender yet crisp.

4 Add the dressing to the salmon, toss together gently and cook for 30 seconds. Remove the pan from the heat.

5 Arrange the salad leaves on serving plates. Drain the beans and toss over the leaves. Spoon over the salmon and cooking juices and serve immediately, sprinkled with the sesame seeds.

RED SNAPPER WITH FENNEL

Whole red-skinned fish, such as snapper, are excellent cooked in this way – you'll need only two fish if they are large.

INGREDIENTS

Serves 4

3 small fennel bulbs
4 tbsp olive oil
2 small onions, thinly sliced
2–4 basil leaves
4 small or 2 large red snapper, cleaned
grated rind of ½ lemon
⅔ cup fish stock
4 tbsp butter
juice of 1 lemon

1 Snip off the feathery fronds from the fennel, finely chop and reserve for the garnish. Cut the fennel into wedges, leaving the layers attached at the root ends so the pieces stay intact.

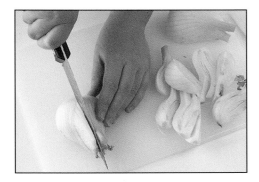

2 Heat the oil in a frying pan large enough to take the fish in a single layer. Add the wedges of fennel and the onions and cook for 10–15 minutes, until softened and lightly browned.

3 Tuck a basil leaf inside each fish, then place on top of the vegetables. Sprinkle over the lemon rind. Pour in the stock and bring just to a boil. Cover and cook gently for 15–20 minutes, until the fish is tender.

4 Melt the butter in a small pan and, when it starts to sizzle and color slightly, add the lemon juice. Pour over the snapper, sprinkle with the reserved fennel fronds and serve.

Char-Broiled Squid

Ingredients

Serves 4

2lb squid, cleaned
6 tbsp olive oil
juice of 1–2 lemons
3 garlic cloves, crushed
¼ tsp hot red pepper flakes
4 tbsp chopped fresh parsley
lemon slices, to garnish

1 Reserve the squid tentacles, then using a small sharp knife, score the flesh into a diagonal pattern.

2 Place all the squid in a shallow non-metallic dish. To make the marinade, mix together the olive oil, lemon juice, crushed garlic and hot red pepper flakes in a small bowl.

3 Pour the marinade over the squid and leave in a cool place for at least 2 hours, stirring occasionally.

4 Lift the squid from the marinade and grill for 2 minutes on each side, turning them frequently and brushing with the marinade until the outside is golden brown and crisp, with soft, moist flesh inside.

5 Bring the remaining marinade to a boil in a small pan, stir in the chopped parsley, then pour over the squid. Garnish with lemon slices and serve at once.

> COOK'S TIP
> If you are in a rush, it is still worth marinating the squid – even for 20 minutes – as this will both tenderize and flavor it.

Monkfish Brochettes

Ingredients

Serves 4

1½lb monkfish, skinned and boned
12 rashers lean bacon
2 small zucchini
1 yellow or orange bell pepper, seeded and cut into 1in cubes

For the marinade

6 tbsp olive oil
grated rind of ½ lime
3 tbsp lime juice
2 tbsp dry white wine
4 tbsp chopped fresh mixed herbs, such as dill, chives and parsley
1 tsp honey
black pepper
saffron rice, to serve

1 To make the marinade, mix together the olive oil, lime rind and juice, wine, chopped herbs, honey and pepper in a bowl, then set aside.

2 Cut the monkfish into 24 x 1in cubes. Stretch the bacon rashers with the back of a knife, then cut each piece in half and wrap around the monkfish cubes.

3 Pare narrow strips of peel from the zucchini to give a striped effect, then cut into 1in chunks.

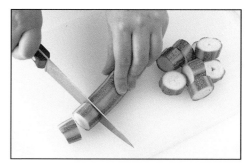

4 Thread the fish rolls on to skewers alternately with the zucchini and pepper. Place in a dish. Pour over the marinade and leave in a cool place for 1 hour. Lift out the skewers, then grill for about 10 minutes, turning and basting occasionally with the marinade. Serve hot with saffron rice.

TUNA WITH PAN-FRIED TOMATOES

Serves 2

2 tuna steaks, about 6oz each
6 tbsp olive oil
2 tbsp lemon juice
2 garlic cloves, chopped
1 tsp chopped fresh thyme
4 canned anchovy fillets, drained and
* finely chopped*
8oz plum tomatoes, halved
2 tbsp chopped fresh parsley
4 – 6 black olives, pitted and chopped
black pepper
crusty bread, to serve

COOK'S TIP

If you are unable to find fresh tuna steaks, you could replace them with salmon fillets, if you like – just cook them for one or two minutes more on each side.

---

1 Place the tuna steaks in a shallow non-metallic dish. Mix 4 tbsp of the oil with the lemon juice, garlic, thyme, anchovies and pepper. Pour this mixture over the tuna and then leave to marinate for at least 1 hour.

2 Lift the tuna from the marinade and place on a broiling rack. Broil for 4 minutes on each side, or until the tuna feels firm to touch, basting with the marinade. Take care not to overcook.

3 Meanwhile, heat the remaining oil in a frying pan. Add the tomatoes and fry for 2 minutes only on each side.

4 Divide the tomatoes equally between two serving plates and scatter over the chopped parsley and olives. Top each with a tuna steak.

5 Add the remaining marinade to the pan juices and warm through. Pour over the tomatoes and tuna steaks and serve at once with crusty bread for mopping up the juices.

SAUTÉED SALMON WITH CUCUMBER

Cucumber is the classic accompaniment to salmon. Here it is served hot – be careful not to overcook the cucumber, or the texture will be lost.

INGREDIENTS

Serves 4

1lb salmon fillet, skinned
3 tbsp butter
2 scallions, chopped
½ cucumber, seeded and cut into strips
4 tbsp dry white wine
½ cup crème fraîche or heavy cream
2 tbsp snipped fresh chives
2 tomatoes, peeled, seeded and diced
salt and black pepper

1 Cut the salmon into about 12 thin slices, then cut across into strips.

2 Melt the butter in a large sauté pan, add the salmon and sauté for 1–2 minutes. Remove the salmon strips using a slotted spoon and set aside.

3 Add the scallions to the pan and cook for 2 minutes. Stir in the cucumber and sauté for 1–2 minutes, until hot. Remove the cucumber and keep warm with the salmon.

4 Add the wine to the pan and let it bubble until well reduced. Stir in the cucumber, crème fraîche or cream, 1 tbsp of the chives and seasoning. Return the salmon to the pan and warm gently. Sprinkle over the tomatoes and remaining chives. Serve at once.

BABY LEAF SALAD WITH CROÛTONS

INGREDIENTS

Serves 4

1 tbsp olive oil
1 garlic clove, crushed
1 tbsp freshly grated Parmesan or
    Romano cheese
1 tbsp chopped fresh parsley
4 slices ciabatta bread, crusts removed,
    cut into small cubes
1 large bunch watercress
large handful of arugula
1 bag mixed baby salad leaves, includ-
    ing oak leaf and Romaine lettuce
1 ripe avocado

For the dressing
3 tbsp olive oil
1 tbsp walnut oil
juice of ½ lemon
½ tsp Dijon mustard
salt and black pepper

1 Preheat the oven to 375°F. Put the oil, garlic, Parmesan, parsley and bread in a bowl and toss to coat well. Spread out the bread cubes on a baking sheet and bake for about 8 minutes until crisp. Leave to cool.

2 Remove any coarse or discolored stalks or leaves from the watercress and place in a serving bowl with the arugula and baby salad leaves.

3 Halve the avocado and remove the pit. Peel and cut into chunks, then add it to the salad bowl.

4 To make the dressing, mix together the oils, lemon juice, mustard and seasoning in a small bowl or screw-topped jar until evenly blended. Pour over the salad and toss well. Sprinkle over the croûtons and serve at once.

WILD RICE WITH BROILED VEGETABLES

Broiling brings out the flavor of these summer vegetables.

INGREDIENTS

Serves 4

1⅓ cups wild and long grain rice
    mixture
1 large eggplant, thickly sliced
1 red, 1 yellow and 1 green bell pepper,
    seeded and cut into quarters
2 red onions, sliced
8oz cremini or shiitake mushrooms
2 small zucchini, cut in half
    lengthwise
olive oil, for brushing
2 tbsp chopped fresh thyme

For the dressing
6 tbsp extra virgin olive oil
2 tbsp balsamic vinegar
2 garlic cloves, crushed
salt and black pepper

1 Put the wild and long grain rice mixture in a pan of cold salted water. Bring to a boil, then reduce the heat, cover and cook gently for 30–40 minutes (or follow the packet instructions), until the grains are tender.

2 To make the dressing, mix together the olive oil, vinegar, garlic and seasoning in a bowl or screw-topped jar until well blended. Set aside while you grill the vegetables.

3 Arrange the vegetables on a broiling rack. Brush with olive oil and broil for 8–10 minutes, until tender and well browned, turning them occasionally and brushing again with oil.

4 Drain the rice and toss in half the dressing. Tip into a serving dish and arrange the broiled vegetables on top. Pour over the remaining dressing and scatter over the chopped thyme.

POTATO AND RED PEPPER FRITTATA

Fresh herbs make all the difference in this simple but delicious recipe – parsley or chives could be substituted for the chopped mint.

INGREDIENTS

Serves 3–4
1lb small new potatoes
6 eggs
2 tbsp chopped fresh mint
2 tbsp olive oil
1 onion, chopped
2 garlic cloves, crushed
2 red bell peppers, seeded and roughly chopped
salt and black pepper
mint sprigs, to garnish

1 Scrub the potatoes, then cook in a pan of boiling salted water until just tender. Drain the potatoes, leave to cool slightly, then cut into thick slices.

2 Whisk together the eggs, mint and seasoning in a bowl, then set aside. Heat the oil in a large frying pan.

3 Add the onion, garlic, peppers and potatoes to the pan and cook, stirring, for 5 minutes.

4 Pour the egg mixture over the vegetables and stir gently.

5 Push the mixture into the center of the pan as it cooks to allow the liquid egg to run on to the base.

6 Once the egg mixture is lightly set, place the pan under a hot broiler for 2–3 minutes, until golden brown. Serve hot or cold, cut into wedges and garnished with sprigs of mint.

RED ONION GALETTES

For a non-vegetarian version, scatter some chopped anchovies over the galettes before baking.

INGREDIENTS

Serves 4
4–5 tbsp olive oil
1¼ lb red onions, sliced
1 garlic clove, crushed
2 tbsp chopped fresh mixed herbs, such as thyme, parsley and basil
8oz ready-made puff pastry
1 tbsp sun-dried tomato paste
black pepper
thyme sprigs, to garnish

1 Heat 2 tbsp of the oil in a pan and add the onions and garlic. Cover and cook gently for 15–20 minutes, stirring occasionally, until soft but not browned. Stir in the herbs.

2 Preheat the oven to 425°F. Divide the pastry into four equal pieces and roll out each one to a 6in round. Flute the edges and prick all over with a fork. Place on baking sheets and chill for about 10 minutes.

3 Mix 1 tbsp of the remaining olive oil with the sun-dried tomato paste and brush over the centers of the rounds, leaving a ½ in border.

4 Spread the onion mixture over the pastry rounds and grind over plenty of pepper. Drizzle over a little more oil, then bake for about 15 minutes, until the pastry is crisp and golden. Serve hot, garnished with thyme sprigs.

SPAGHETTI WITH HERB SAUCE

Herbs make a wonderfully aromatic sauce – the heat from the pasta releases their flavor to delicious effect.

— INGREDIENTS —

Serves 4

2oz chopped fresh mixed herbs, such as
    parsley, basil and thyme
2 garlic cloves, crushed
4 tbsp pine nuts, toasted
⅔ cup olive oil
12oz dried spaghetti
4 tbsp freshly grated Parmesan cheese
salt and black pepper
basil leaves, to garnish

1 Put the herbs, garlic and half the pine nuts into a food processor. With the machine running slowly, add the oil and process to form a thick purée.

2 Cook the spaghetti in plenty of boiling salted water for 8 minutes until *al dente*. Drain thoroughly.

3 Transfer the herb purée to a large warm bowl, then add the spaghetti and Parmesan. Toss well to coat the pasta with the sauce. Sprinkle over the remaining pine nuts and the basil leaves and serve immediately.

CHIVE OMELETTE STIR-FRY

Sesame oil has a lovely aroma and a distinctive toasted flavor. It is often added to oriental dishes at the last moment.

— INGREDIENTS —

Serves 3–4

2 celery stalks
2 carrots
2 small zucchini
4 scallions
1 bunch radishes
2 eggs
1–2 tbsp snipped fresh chives
2 tbsp groundnut oil
1 garlic clove, chopped
½ in piece fresh ginger root, chopped
4oz bean sprouts
¼ head of Chinese cabbage, shredded
sesame oil, to taste
salt and black pepper

1 Cut the celery, carrots, zucchini and scallions into fine shreds. Trim the radishes, slice into rounds, then cut the rounds in half. Set aside.

2 Whisk together the eggs, chives and seasoning in a bowl. Heat 1 tsp of the groundnut oil in an omelette pan and pour in just enough of the egg mixture to cover the base of the pan. Cook for about 1 minute until set, then turn over the omelette and cook for a further minute.

3 Tip out the omelette on to a plate and cook the rest of the egg mixture in the same way to make several omelettes, adding extra oil to the pan, if necessary. Roll up each omelette and slice thinly. Keep the omelettes warm in a low oven until required.

4 Heat the remaining oil in a wok or large frying pan, add the chopped garlic and ginger and stir-fry for a few seconds to flavor the oil.

5 Add the shredded celery, carrots and zucchini and stir-fry for 1 minute. Add the radishes, bean sprouts, scallions and Chinese cabbage and stir-fry for 2–3 minutes, until the vegetables are tender but still crunchy. Sprinkle a little sesame oil over the vegetables and toss gently.

6 Serve the stir-fried vegetables at once with the sliced chive omelettes scattered over the top.

TWICE-BAKED CHEDDAR SOUFFLÉS

This is an ace of a recipe for busy people and really easy to make. The soufflés can be prepared well in advance, then simply reheated just before serving.

Serves 4
1¼ cups milk
flavoring ingredients (a few onion slices, 1 bay leaf and 4 black peppercorns)
5 tbsp butter
⅓ cup flour
4oz sharp Cheddar cheese, grated
¼ tsp mustard powder
3 eggs, separated
4 tsp chopped fresh parsley
1 cup heavy cream
salt and black pepper

1 Preheat the oven to 350°F. Put the milk in a pan with the flavoring ingredients. Bring slowly to a boil, then strain into a cup.

> **COOK'S TIP**
> Don't attempt to unmould the soufflés until they have cooled, when they will be firmer and easier to handle. They can be kept chilled for up to 8 hours. Use snipped fresh chives instead of the parsley, if you like.

2 Melt the butter in the rinsed-out pan and use a little to grease four ¼ pint/⅔ cup ramekins.

3 Stir the flour into the remaining butter in the pan and cook for 1 minute. Gradually add the hot milk, then bring to a boil, stirring until thickened and smooth. Cook, stirring all the time, for 2 minutes.

4 Remove the pan from the heat and stir in 3oz of the grated cheese and the mustard powder. Beat in the egg yolks, followed by the chopped parsley, and season to taste with salt and plenty of black pepper.

5 Whisk the egg whites in a large bowl until stiff but not dry. Mix in a spoonful of the egg whites to lighten the cheese mixture, then gently fold in the remaining egg whites.

6 Spoon the soufflé mixture into the ramekins, place in a roasting pan and pour in boiling water to come halfway up the sides. Bake the soufflés for 15–20 minutes until risen and set. Remove the ramekins immediately from the roasting pan and allow the soufflés to sink and cool, until ready to serve.

7 When ready to serve, preheat the oven to 425°F. Carefully turn out the soufflés into a buttered shallow ovenproof dish or individual dishes. Season the cream and pour over the soufflés, then sprinkle over the remaining cheese.

8 Bake the soufflés for about 10–15 minutes, until risen and golden brown. Serve at once.

STRAWBERRY AND BLUEBERRY TART

This tart works equally well using either autumn or winter fruits as long as there is a riot of color and the fruit is in perfect condition.

INGREDIENTS

Serves 6–8
2 cups flour
pinch of salt
9 tbsp confectioners' sugar
10 tbsp unsalted butter, diced
1 egg yolk

For the filling
1¼ cups mascarpone
2 tbsp confectioners' sugar
few drops vanilla extract
finely grated rind of 1 orange
1–1½lb fresh mixed strawberries
    and blueberries
6 tbsp red currant jelly
2 tbsp orange juice

1 Sift the flour, salt and sugar into a bowl, and rub in the butter until the mixture resembles coarse crumbs. Using a round-bladed knife, mix in the egg yolk and 2 tsp cold water. Gather the dough together, then turn out on to a floured surface and knead lightly until smooth. Wrap and chill for 1 hour.

2 Preheat the oven to 375°F. Roll out the pastry and use to line a 10in fluted quiche pan. Prick the base and chill for 15 minutes.

3 Line the chilled pastry case with wax paper and baking beans, then bake for 15 minutes. Remove the paper and beans and bake for a further 15 minutes, until crisp and golden. Leave to cool in the pan.

4 Beat together the mascarpone, sugar, vanilla extract and orange rind in a mixing bowl until smooth.

5 Tip the pastry case out of the pan, then spoon in the filling and pile the fruits on top. Heat the red currant jelly with the orange juice until runny, sieve, then brush over the fruit to glaze.

CHOCOLATE AMARETTI PEACHES

Quick and easy to prepare, this delicious dessert can also be made with fresh nectarines or apricots.

INGREDIENTS

Serves 4
4oz amaretti cookies, crushed
2oz semisweet chocolate, chopped
grated rind of ½ orange
1 tbsp honey
¼ tsp ground cinnamon
1 egg white, lightly beaten
4 firm ripe peaches
⅔ cup white wine
1 tbsp sugar
whipped cream, to serve

1 Preheat the oven to 375°F. Mix together the crushed amaretti cookies, chocolate, orange rind, honey and cinnamon in a bowl. Add the beaten egg white and then mix to bind the mixture together.

2 Halve and pit the peaches and fill the cavities with the chocolate mixture, mounding it up slightly.

3 Arrange the stuffed peaches in a lightly buttered, shallow ovenproof dish which will just hold the peaches comfortably. Pour the wine into a measuring cup and stir in the sugar.

4 Pour the wine mixture around the peaches. Bake for 30–40 minutes, until the peaches are tender. Serve at once with a little of the cooking juices spooned over and the whipped cream.

CHERRIES JUBILEE

Fresh cherries are wonderful cooked lightly to serve hot over ice cream. Children especially will love this dessert.

─────── INGREDIENTS ───────

Serves 4

1lb red or black cherries
½ cup sugar
pared rind of 1 lemon
1 tbsp arrowroot
4 tbsp Kirsch
vanilla ice cream, to serve

┌─────────────────────────────┐
│ COOK'S TIP   │
│ If you don't have a cherry   │
│ pitter, simply push the   │
│ stones through with a   │
│ skewer. Remember to save   │
│ the juice for the recipe.   │
└─────────────────────────────┘

1 Pit the cherries over a pan to catch the juice. Drop the pits into the pan as you work.

2 Add the sugar, lemon rind and 1¼ cups water to the pan. Stir over a low heat until the sugar dissolves, then bring to a boil and simmer for 10 minutes. Strain the syrup, then return to the pan. Add the cherries and cook for 3–4 minutes.

3 Blend the arrowroot to a paste with 1 tbsp cold water and stir into the cherries, off the heat.

4 Return the pan to the heat and bring to a boil, stirring all the time. Cook the sauce for a minute or two, stirring until it is thick and smooth. Heat the Kirsch in a ladle over a flame, ignite and pour over the cherries. Spoon the hot sauce over scoops of ice cream and serve at once.

APRICOTS IN MARSALA

Make sure the apricots are completely covered by the syrup so that they don't discolor.

─────── INGREDIENTS ───────

Serves 4

12 apricots
4 tbsp sugar
1¼ cups Marsala
2 strips pared orange rind
1 vanilla pod, split
⅔ cup heavy or whipping
  cream
1 tbsp confectioners' sugar
¼ tsp ground cinnamon
⅔ cup strained plain yogurt

1 Halve and pit the apricots, then place in a bowl of boiling water for about 30 seconds. Drain well, then carefully slip off their skins.

2 Place the sugar, Marsala, orange rind, vanilla pod and 1 cup water in a pan. Heat gently until the sugar dissolves. Bring to a boil, without stirring, then simmer for 2–3 minutes.

3 Add the apricot halves to the pan and poach them for about 5–6 minutes, or until they are just tender. Using a slotted spoon, transfer the apricots to a serving dish.

4 Boil the syrup rapidly until reduced by half, then pour over the apricots and leave to cool. Cover and chill for several hours. Remove the orange rind and vanilla pod.

5 Whip the cream with the confectioners' sugar and cinnamon until it forms soft peaks. Gently fold in the yogurt. Spoon into a serving bowl and chill until required. Serve with the apricots.

SUMMER BERRY MEDLEY

Make the most of glorious seasonal fruits in this refreshing dessert. The sauce is also good swirled into plain or strawberry-flavored yogurt.

INGREDIENTS

Serves 4–6
6oz red currants
6oz raspberries
4 tbsp sugar
2–3 tbsp raspberry liqueur
1–1½lb mixed soft summer
fruits, such as strawberries, raspberries,
  blueberries, red currants and
  black currants
vanilla ice cream, to serve

1 Strip the red currants from their stalks using a fork and place in a bowl with the raspberries, sugar and raspberry liqueur. Cover and leave to macerate for 1–2 hours.

2 Put this fruit with its macerating juices in a pan and cook gently for 5–6 minutes, stirring occasionally, until the fruit is just tender.

3 Pour the fruit into a blender or food processor and blend until smooth. Press through a nylon sieve to remove any seeds. Leave to cool, then chill.

4 Divide the mixed soft fruit among four individual glass serving dishes and pour over the sauce. Serve with scoops of vanilla ice cream.

BROWN BREAD ICE CREAM

───── INGREDIENTS ─────

Serves 6
½ cup roasted and chopped hazelnuts,
    ground
1½ cups whole wheat bread crumbs
4 tbsp raw sugar
3 egg whites
½ cup sugar
1¼ cups heavy cream
few drops vanilla extract

For the sauce
8oz black currants
6 tbsp sugar
1 tbsp crème de cassis
fresh mint sprigs, to decorate

1 Combine the hazelnuts and bread crumbs on a baking sheet, then sprinkle over the raw sugar. Place under a medium broiler and cook, stirring, until the mixture is crisp and evenly browned. Leave to cool.

2 Whisk the egg whites in a bowl until stiff, then gradually whisk in the sugar until thick and glossy. Whip the cream until it forms soft peaks and fold into the meringue with the bread crumb mixture and vanilla extract.

3 Spoon the mixture into a 5 cup loaf pan. Smooth the top level, then cover and freeze for several hours, or until firm.

4 Meanwhile, make the sauce. Strip the black currants from their stalks using a fork and put them in a small bowl with the sugar. Toss gently to mix and leave for 30 minutes.

5 Purée the black currants in a blender or food processor, then press through a nylon sieve until smooth. Add the crème de cassis and chill well.

6 To serve, turn out the ice cream on to a plate and cut into slices. Arrange each slice on a serving plate, spoon over a little sauce and decorate with fresh mint sprigs.

RASPBERRY MERINGUE GÂTEAU

A rich, hazelnut meringue filled with cream and raspberries makes a wonderful dessert served with a raspberry sauce.

INGREDIENTS

Serves 6
4 egg whites
1 cup sugar
few drops vanilla extract
1 tsp distilled malt vinegar
1 cup roasted and chopped hazelnuts,
*   ground*
1¼ cups heavy cream
12oz raspberries
confectioners' sugar, for dusting
raspberries and mint sprigs,
*   to decorate*

For the sauce
8oz raspberries
3–4 tbsp confectioners' sugar,
*   sifted*
1 tbsp orange liqueur

1 Preheat the oven to 350°F. Grease two 8in shallow cake pans and line the bases with rounds of wax paper.

2 Whisk the egg whites in a large bowl until they hold stiff peaks, then gradually whisk in the caster sugar a tablespoon at a time, whisking well after each addition.

3 Continue whisking the meringue mixture for a minute or two until very stiff, then fold in the vanilla extract, vinegar and ground hazelnuts.

4 Divide the meringue mixture between the prepared cake pans and spread level. Bake for about 50–60 minutes, until crisp. Remove the meringues from the pans and leave to cool on a wire rack.

5 While the meringues are cooling, make the sauce. Purée the raspberries with the confectioners' sugar and orange liqueur in a blender or food processor, then press the purée through a fine nylon strainer to remove any seeds. Chill the sauce until ready to serve.

COOK'S TIP
You can buy roasted chopped hazelnuts in supermarkets. Otherwise toast whole hazelnuts under the broiler and rub off the flaky skins using a clean dish towel. To chop finely, whizz in a food processor for a few moments.

6 Whip the cream until it forms soft peaks, then gently fold in the raspberries. Sandwich the meringue rounds together with the raspberry cream.

7 Dust the top of the gâteau with confectioners' sugar. Decorate with raspberries and mint sprigs and serve with the raspberry sauce.

VARIATION
Fresh red currants make a good alternative to raspberries. Pick over the fruit, then pull each sprig gently through the prongs of a fork to release the red currants. Add them to the whipped cream with a little sugar, to taste.

AUTUMN

Cooler days bring with them the first hint of autumn, and an abundance of blackberries, plums, apples and pears which make lovely desserts like Pear and Blueberry Pie, Plum and Port Mousse, and Blackberry Brown Sugar Meringue. Vegetables such as parsnips, onions, turnips, rutabaga, beet and pumpkins are in good supply and you may also be lucky in finding field mushrooms for making Mushroom and Pancetta Pizzas, and Trout with Mushroom Cream Sauce. Game is back in season and Normandy Pheasant makes the perfect dinner-party dish. There is also a steadily improving selection of fish and shellfish. Look out for herring, skate and hake, and what could be better than a bowl of Tagliatelle with Saffron Mussels? Take advantage too, of hazelnuts – just right for dishes like Iced Chocolate and Nut Gâteau.

SPICED PARSNIP SOUP

This pale creamy-textured soup is given a special touch with an aromatic, spiced garlic and coriander garnish.

INGREDIENTS

Serves 4–6
3 tbsp butter
1 onion, chopped
1½lb parsnips, diced
1 tsp ground coriander
½ tsp ground cumin
½ tsp ground turmeric
¼ tsp chili powder
5 cups chicken stock
⅔ cup light cream
1 tbsp sunflower oil
1 garlic clove, cut into julienne strips
2 tsp yellow mustard seeds
salt and black pepper

1 Melt the butter in a large pan, add the onion and parsnips and fry gently for about 3 minutes.

2 Stir in the spices and cook for 1 minute more. Add the stock, season and bring to a boil, then reduce the heat. Cover and simmer for about 45 minutes, until the parsnips are tender.

3 Cool slightly, then purée in a blender until smooth. Return the soup to the pan, add the cream and heat through gently over a low heat.

4 Heat the oil in a small pan, add the julienne strips of garlic and yellow mustard seeds and fry quickly until the garlic is beginning to brown and the mustard seeds start to pop and splutter. Remove the pan from the heat.

5 Ladle the soup into warmed soup bowls and pour a little of the hot spice mixture over each. Serve at once.

PUMPKIN SOUP

The flavor of this soup develops if it is made a day in advance.

─── INGREDIENTS ───

Serves 4–6
2lb pumpkin
3 tbsp olive oil
2 onions, chopped
2 celery stalks, chopped
1lb tomatoes, chopped
6 cups vegetable stock
2 tbsp tomato paste
1 bouquet garni
*2–3 rashers lean bacon, crisply fried
    and crumbled*
2 tbsp chopped fresh parsley
salt and black pepper

1 Cut the pumpkin into thin slices, discarding the skin and seeds.

2 Heat the oil in a large pan and fry the onions and celery for about 5 minutes. Add the pumpkin and tomatoes and cook for a further 5 minutes.

3 Add the vegetable stock, tomato paste, bouquet garni and seasoning to the pan. Bring the soup to a boil, then reduce the heat, cover the pan and simmer for about 45 minutes.

4 Allow the soup to cool slightly, remove the bouquet garni, then purée (in two batches, if necessary) in a blender or food processor.

5 Press the soup through a strainer, then return it to the pan. Reheat the soup gently and season to taste.

6 Ladle the soup into warmed soup bowls. Sprinkle with the crispy bacon and parsley and serve at once.

BEET AND HERRING SALAD

This colorful salad uses fresh beets. This delicious vegetable is too often underrated.

INGREDIENTS

Serves 4
12oz cooked beets, skinned and thickly
  sliced
2 tbsp vinaigrette dressing
4 pickled herrings, drained
12oz cooked waxy salad potatoes,
  thickly sliced
½ small red onion, thinly sliced and
  separated
⅔ cup sour cream
2 tbsp snipped fresh chives
dark rye bread, to serve

1 Mix the sliced beets with the vinaigrette dressing. Arrange the herrings on individual plates with the beets, potatoes and onion rings.

2 Add a generous spoonful of the sour cream to each serving and sprinkle with snipped fresh chives. Serve with dark rye bread.

GARLIC SHRIMP IN FILO TARTLETS

Tartlets made with crisp layers of filo pastry and filled with garlic shrimp make a tempting and unusual dinner-party appetizer.

INGREDIENTS

Serves 4
For the tartlets
4 tbsp butter, melted
2–3 large sheets filo pastry

For the filling
½ cup butter
2–3 garlic cloves, crushed
1 red chili, seeded and chopped
12oz cooked, peeled shrimp
2 tbsp chopped fresh parsley or
  snipped fresh chives
salt and black pepper

1 Preheat the oven to 400°F. Brush four individual 3in pie pans with melted butter.

2 Cut the filo pastry into twelve 4in squares and brush them with the melted butter.

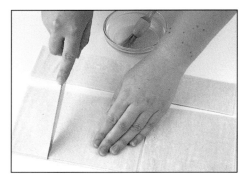

3 Place three squares inside each pan, overlapping them at slight angles and carefully frilling the edges and points while forming a good hollow in each center. Bake for 10–15 minutes, until crisp and golden. Cool slightly and remove from the pans.

4 Meanwhile, make the filling. Melt the butter in a large frying pan, then add the garlic, chili and shrimp and fry quickly for 1–2 minutes to warm through. Stir in the parsley or chives and season with salt and pepper.

5 Spoon the shrimp filling into the tartlets and serve at once.

COOK'S TIP
Use fresh filo pastry, rather than frozen, then simply wrap and freeze any leftover sheets.

MUSHROOM AND PANCETTA PIZZAS

Serves 4
For the base
2 cups flour
½ tsp salt
1 tsp fast-rising dried yeast
2 tbsp olive oil

For the topping
4 tbsp olive oil
2 garlic cloves, crushed
8oz fresh porcini or cremini
  mushrooms, roughly chopped
3oz pancetta, roughly chopped
1 tbsp chopped fresh oregano
3 tbsp grated Parmesan cheese
salt and black pepper

1 To make the base, put the flour, salt and yeast into a food processor and process for a few seconds. Measure ⅔ cup warm water into a cup and add the olive oil. With the machine running, add the liquid until the mixture forms a soft dough.

2 Turn out the dough on to a lightly floured surface and knead until smooth and elastic. Place in an oiled bowl and cover with plastic wrap. Leave the dough in a warm place for about 1 hour until doubled in size.

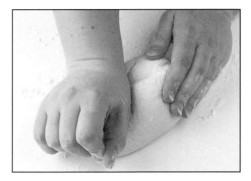

3 Turn out the dough on to a floured surface and divide into four pieces.

4 Roll out each piece of dough thinly to a 5in round. Place the pizza bases on a lightly greased baking sheet and set aside.

5 Preheat the oven to 425°F. Heat 2 tbsp of the olive oil in a frying pan. Add the garlic and mushrooms and fry gently until the mushrooms are tender and the juices have evaporated. Season, then cool.

6 Brush the pizza bases with about 1 tbsp oil, then spoon over the mushrooms. Scatter over the pancetta and oregano. Sprinkle with Parmesan and drizzle over the remaining oil. Bake for 10–15 minutes, until crisp.

COOK'S TIP
Look out for pancetta in major supermarkets and Italian delis. If you can't find it, thickly sliced bacon may be used instead.

BLINIS WITH SMOKED SALMON AND DILL

Serves 4
1 cup buckwheat flour
1 cup flour
pinch of salt
1 tbsp fast-rising dried yeast
2 eggs
1½ cups warm milk
1 tbsp melted butter, plus extra
    for frying
⅔ cup crème fraîche or sour cream
3 tbsp chopped fresh dill
8oz smoked salmon, thinly
    sliced
fresh dill sprigs, to garnish

1 Mix together the two flours in a large bowl with the salt. Sprinkle in the yeast and mix well. Separate one of the eggs. Whisk together the whole egg and the yolk, the warm milk and the melted butter.

2 Pour the egg mixture on to the flour mixture. Beat well to form a batter. Cover with plastic wrap and leave to rise in a warm place for 1–2 hours.

3 Whisk the remaining egg white in a large bowl until it holds stiff peaks, then gently fold into the batter.

4 Preheat a heavy-based frying pan or griddle and brush with melted butter. Drop tablespoons of the batter on to the pan, spacing them well apart. Cook for about 40 seconds, until bubbles appear on the surface.

5 Flip over the blinis and cook for 30 seconds on the other side. Wrap in foil and keep warm in a low oven. Repeat with the remaining mixture, buttering the pan each time.

6 Mix together the crème fraîche and dill. Serve the blinis topped with the smoked salmon and dill cream. Garnish with sprigs of fresh dill.

SPICED LAMB WITH APRICOTS

Serves 4

½ cup ready-to-eat dried apricots
⅓ cup seedless raisins
½ tsp saffron strands
⅔ cup orange juice
1 tbsp red wine vinegar
2–3 tbsp olive oil
3lb leg of lamb, boned and
   cubed
1 onion, chopped
2 garlic cloves, crushed
2 tsp ground cumin
¼ tsp ground cloves
1 tbsp ground coriander
2 tbsp flour
2½ cups lamb stock
3 tbsp chopped fresh coriander
salt and black pepper
saffron rice mixed with toasted
   almonds and chopped fresh
   coriander, to serve

1 Mix together the dried apricots, raisins, saffron, orange juice and vinegar in a bowl. Cover and leave to soak for 2–3 hours.

2 Preheat the oven to 325°F. Heat 2 tbsp oil in a large flameproof casserole and brown the lamb in batches. Remove and set aside. Add the onion and garlic with a little more of the remaining oil, if necessary, and cook until softened.

3 Stir in the spices and flour and cook for a further 1–2 minutes. Return the meat to the casserole. Stir in the stock, fresh coriander and the soaked fruit with its liquid. Add seasoning, then bring to a boil.

4 Cover the casserole and cook for 1½ hours (adding a little extra stock if necessary), or until the lamb is tender. Serve with saffron rice mixed with toasted almonds and fresh coriander.

SAUSAGE AND BEAN RAGOÛT

An economical and nutritious main course that children will love. Garlic and herb bread makes an ideal accompaniment.

Serves 4

2 cups dried cannellini or flageolet
   beans, soaked overnight
3 tbsp olive oil
1 onion, finely chopped
2 garlic cloves, crushed
1lb good-quality chunky sausages,
   skinned and thickly sliced
1 tbsp tomato paste
2 tbsp fresh chopped parsley
1 tbsp fresh chopped thyme
14oz can chopped tomatoes
salt and black pepper
chopped fresh thyme and parsley,
to garnish

1 Drain and rinse the soaked beans and place them in a pan with enough water to cover. Bring to a boil, cover the pan and simmer for about 1 hour, or until tender. Drain the beans and set aside.

2 Heat the oil and fry the onion, garlic and sausages until golden.

3 Stir in the tomato paste, chopped parsley and thyme, tomatoes and seasoning, then bring to a boil.

4 Add the beans, then cover and cook gently for about 15 minutes, stirring occasionally, until the sausages are cooked through. Garnish with extra chopped fresh herbs and serve.

BEEF PAPRIKA WITH ROASTED PEPPERS

This dish is perfect for family suppers – roasting the peppers gives a new dimension.

INGREDIENTS

Serves 4
2 tbsp olive oil
1½lb chuck steak, cut into 1½in cubes
2 onions, chopped
1 garlic clove, crushed
1 tbsp flour
1 tbsp paprika, plus extra to
  garnish
14oz can chopped tomatoes
2 red bell peppers, halved and seeded
⅔ cup crème fraîche or sour cream
salt and black pepper
buttered noodles, to serve

1 Preheat the oven to 275°F. Heat the oil in a large flameproof casserole and brown the meat in batches. Remove the meat from the casserole using a slotted spoon.

2 Add the onions and garlic and fry gently until softened. Stir in the flour and paprika and continue cooking for a further 1–2 minutes, stirring.

3 Return the meat and any juices that have collected on the plate to the casserole, then add the chopped tomatoes and seasoning. Bring to a boil, stirring, then cover and cook in the oven for 2½ hours.

4 Meanwhile, place the peppers skin-side up on a broiling rack and broil until the skins have blistered and charred. Cool, then peel off the skins. Cut the flesh into strips. Add to the casserole and cook for a further 15–30 minutes, or until the meat is tender.

5 Stir in the crème fraîche or sour cream and sprinkle with paprika. Serve hot with buttered noodles.

> **COOK'S TIP**
> Take care when browning the meat and add only a few pieces at a time. If you overcrowd the pan, steam is created and the meat will never brown!

PEPPERED STEAKS WITH MADEIRA

A really easy special-occasion dish. Mixed peppercorns have an excellent flavor, though black pepper will, of course, do instead.

INGREDIENTS

Serves 4

1 tbsp mixed dried peppercorns (green, pink and black)
4 fillet or sirloin steaks, about 6oz each
1 tbsp olive oil, plus extra for frying
1 garlic clove, crushed
4 tbsp Madeira
6 tbsp fresh beef stock
⅔ cup heavy cream
salt

1 Finely crush the peppercorns using a pestle and mortar, then press on to both sides of the steaks.

2 Place the steaks in a shallow non-metallic dish, then add the oil, garlic and Madeira. Cover and leave to marinate in a cool place for 4–6 hours, or preferably overnight.

3 Remove the steaks from the dish, reserving the marinade. Brush a little oil over a heavy-based frying pan and heat until hot.

4 Add the steaks and cook over a high heat, allowing 3 minutes per side for medium or 2 minutes per side for rare. Remove and keep warm.

5 Add the reserved marinade and the stock to the pan and bring to the boil, then leave the sauce to bubble until it is well reduced.

6 Add the cream, with salt to taste, to the pan and stir until slightly thickened. Serve the steaks on warmed plates with the sauce.

PASTA WITH CHICKEN LIVERS

Serves 4

*8oz chicken livers, defrosted
    if frozen*
2 tbsp olive oil
2 garlic cloves, crushed
*6oz hickory smoked bacon, coarsely
    chopped*
14oz can chopped tomatoes
⅔ cup chicken stock
1 tbsp tomato paste
1 tbsp dry sherry
*2 tbsp chopped fresh mixed herbs, such
    as parsley, rosemary and basil*
12oz dried orecchiette *pasta*
salt and black pepper
*freshly grated Parmesan cheese,
    to serve*

1 Wash and trim the chicken livers. Cut into bite-sized pieces. Heat the oil in a sauté pan and fry the chicken livers for 3–4 minutes.

2 Add the garlic and bacon to the pan and fry until golden brown. Add the tomatoes, chicken stock, tomato paste, sherry, herbs and seasoning.

3 Bring to a boil and simmer gently, uncovered, for about 5 minutes until the sauce has thickened.

4 Meanwhile, cook the *orecchiette* in boiling salted water for about 12 minutes until *al dente*. Drain well, then toss into the sauce. Serve hot, sprinkled with Parmesan cheese.

> **COOK'S TIP**
> You'll find *orecchiette*, a dried pasta shaped like ears or flying saucers, in most large supermarkets.

CHICKEN BAKED IN A SALT CRUST

This unusual dish is extremely easy to make. Once cooked, you just break away the salt crust to reveal the wonderfully tender, golden brown chicken.

Serves 4

*3–3½lb free-range oven-ready
    chicken*
*bunch of mixed fresh herbs, such
    as rosemary, thyme, marjoram
    and parsley*
*about 3–3½lb/10 cups coarse sea
    salt or kosher salt*
1 egg white
*1–2 whole heads of baked garlic,
    to serve*

1 Wipe the chicken and remove the giblets. Put the herbs into the cavity, then truss the chicken.

2 Mix together the sea salt and egg white until all the salt crystals are moistened. Select a roasting pan into which the chicken will fit neatly, then line it with a large double layer of foil.

3 Spread a thick layer of moistened salt in the foil-lined pan and place the chicken on top. Cover with the remaining salt and press into a neat shape, over and around the chicken, making sure it is completely enclosed.

4 Bring the foil edges up and over the chicken to enclose it and bake in the oven for 1½ hours. Remove from the oven and leave to rest for 10 minutes.

5 Carefully lift the foil package from the container and open. Break the salt crust to reveal the chicken inside. Brush any traces of salt from the bird, then serve with baked whole heads of garlic. Each clove can be slipped from its skin and eaten with a bite of chicken.

FARMHOUSE VENISON PIE

A simple and satisfying pie – venison in a rich gravy, topped with potato and parsnip mash.

INGREDIENTS

Serves 4

3 tbsp sunflower oil
1 onion, chopped
1 garlic clove, crushed
3 rashers lean bacon, chopped
1½lb ground venison
4oz button mushrooms, chopped
2 tbsp flour
1⅞ cups beef stock
⅔ cup ruby port
2 bay leaves
1 tsp chopped fresh thyme
1 tsp Dijon mustard
1 tbsp red currant jelly
1½lb potatoes
1lb parsnips
1 egg yolk
4 tbsp butter
freshly grated nutmeg
3 tbsp chopped fresh parsley
salt and black pepper

1 Heat the oil in a large frying pan and fry the onion, garlic and bacon for about 5 minutes. Add the venison and mushrooms and cook for a few minutes, stirring, until browned.

2 Stir in the flour and cook for 1–2 minutes, then add the stock, port, herbs, mustard, red currant jelly and seasoning. Bring to a boil, cover and simmer for 30–40 minutes, until tender. Spoon into a large pie dish or four individual ovenproof dishes.

3 While the venison and mushroom mixture is cooking, preheat the oven to 400°F. Cut the potatoes and parsnips into large chunks. Cook together in boiling salted water for 20 minutes or until tender. Drain and mash, then beat in the egg yolk, butter, nutmeg, chopped parsley and seasoning.

4 Spread the potato and parsnip mixture over the meat and bake for 30–40 minutes, until piping hot and golden brown. Serve at once.

NORMANDY PHEASANT

Cider, apples and cream make this a rich and flavorful dish.

INGREDIENTS

Serves 4

2 oven-ready pheasants
1 tbsp olive oil
2 tbsp butter
4 tbsp Calvados or Apple Jack
1⅞ cups cider
bouquet garni
3 crisp eating apples, peeled, cored
   and thickly sliced
⅔ cup heavy cream
salt and black pepper
thyme sprigs, to garnish

1 Preheat the oven to 325°F. Joint both pheasants into four pieces using a large sharp knife. Discard the backbones and knuckles.

2 Heat the oil and butter in a large flameproof casserole. Working in two batches, add the pheasant pieces to the casserole and brown them over a high heat. Return all the pheasant pieces to the casserole.

3 Standing well back, pour over the Calvados or Apple Jack and set it alight. When the flames have subsided, pour in the cider, then add the bouquet garni and seasoning and bring to a boil. Cover and cook for 50 minutes.

4 Tuck the apple slices around the pheasant. Cover and cook for 5–10 minutes, or until the pheasant is tender. Transfer the pheasant and apple to a warmed serving plate. Keep warm.

5 Remove the bouquet garni, then reduce the sauce by half to a syrupy consistency. Stir in the cream and simmer for a further 2–3 minutes until thickened. Taste the sauce and adjust the seasoning. Spoon the sauce over the pheasant and serve hot, garnished with thyme sprigs.

SOLE AND PESTO PARCELS

Serve the parcels hot from the oven to the table – the wax paper bakes translucent and looks most attractive.

INGREDIENTS

Serves 4

6 tbsp butter
4 tsp pesto sauce
8 small sole fillets
1 small fennel bulb, cut into matchsticks
2 small carrots, cut into matchsticks
2 zucchini, cut into matchsticks
2 tsp finely grated lemon rind
salt and black pepper
basil leaves, to garnish

1 Preheat the oven to 375°F. Beat 4 tbsp of the butter with the pesto sauce and seasoning to taste. Skin the sole fillets, then spread the pesto butter over the skinned side of each and carefully roll up, starting from the thick end. Set the rolls on one side.

2 Melt the remaining butter in a pan, add the fennel and carrots and sauté for 3 minutes. Add the zucchini and cook for 2 minutes. Remove from the heat. Add the lemon rind and seasoning.

3 Cut four squares of wax paper, each large enough to enclose two fish rolls. Brush with oil. Spoon the vegetables into the center of each, then place two rolls on top.

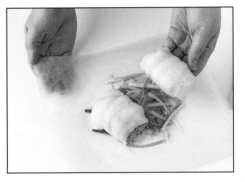

4 Seal the parcels tightly and place in a roasting pan. Bake for 15–20 minutes, until the fish is just tender.

5 To serve, open up the parcels, then sprinkle with the basil leaves and grind over a little black pepper.

SKATE WITH LEMON AND CAPERS

Skate wings served with a sharp, herby sauce make a different – and very easy – main course.

INGREDIENTS

Serves 4

4 small skate wings, about 6–8oz each
seasoned flour
6 tbsp olive oil
1 garlic clove, crushed
finely grated rind of ½ lemon
juice of 1 large lemon
2 tbsp capers, rinsed, drained and chopped
2 tbsp chopped fresh flat leaf parsley
1 tbsp chopped fresh basil
1 tbsp snipped fresh chives
salt and black pepper

1 Lightly dust the skate wings in the seasoned flour. Heat 2 tbsp of the oil in a large frying pan and, when hot, add the skate wings and fry for 8–10 minutes, turning once, until the flesh begins to part easily from the bone and looks creamy white.

2 Meanwhile, mix together the remaining oil, the garlic, lemon rind and juice in a bowl with the capers, parsley, basil, chives and seasoning.

3 Pour the sauce into the pan to warm it through. Transfer the skate to warmed serving plates and serve with the sauce spooned over the top.

TAGLIATELLE WITH SAFFRON MUSSELS

Mussels in a saffron and cream sauce are served with tagliatelle in this recipe, but you can use any other pasta, as you prefer.

INGREDIENTS

Serves 4
4 – 4½lb live mussels
⅔ cup dry white wine
2 shallots, chopped
12oz dried tagliatelle
2 tbsp butter
2 garlic cloves, crushed
1 cup heavy cream
generous pinch of saffron strands
1 egg yolk
salt and black pepper
2 tbsp chopped fresh parsley,
  to garnish

1 Scrub the mussels well under cold running water. Remove the beards and discard any mussels that are open.

2 Place the mussels in a large pan with the wine and shallots. Cover and cook over a high heat, shaking the pan occasionally, for 5 – 8 minutes until the mussels have opened. Drain the mussels, reserving the liquid. Discard any that remain closed. Shell all but a few of the mussels and keep warm.

3 Bring the reserved cooking liquid to a boil, then reduce by half. Strain into a cup to remove any grit.

4 Cook the tagliatelle in a large pan of boiling salted water for about 10 minutes, until *al dente*.

5 Meanwhile, melt the butter in a pan and fry the garlic for 1 minute. Pour in the mussel liquid, cream and saffron strands. Heat gently until the sauce thickens slightly. Remove the pan from the heat and stir in the egg yolk, shelled mussels and seasoning to taste.

6 Drain the tagliatelle and transfer to warmed serving bowls. Spoon the sauce over and sprinkle with chopped parsley. Garnish with the mussels in shells and serve at once.

MONKFISH WITH MEXICAN SALSA

INGREDIENTS

Serves 4
1½lb monkfish tail
3 tbsp olive oil
2 tbsp lime juice
1 garlic clove, crushed
1 tbsp chopped fresh coriander
salt and black pepper
coriander sprigs and lime slices,
  to garnish

For the salsa
4 tomatoes, peeled, seeded and diced
1 avocado, peeled, pitted and diced
½ red onion, chopped
1 green chili, seeded and chopped
2 tbsp chopped fresh coriander
2 tbsp olive oil
1 tbsp lime juice

1 To make the salsa, mix the salsa ingredients and leave at room temperature for about 30 minutes.

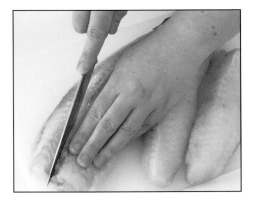

2 Prepare the monkfish. Using a sharp knife, remove the pinkish-grey membrane. Cut the fillets from either side of the backbone, then cut each fillet in half to give four steaks.

3 Mix together the oil, lime juice, garlic, coriander and seasoning in a shallow non-metallic dish. Add the monkfish steaks to the dish. Turn the monkfish several times to coat with the marinade, then cover the dish and leave to marinate at cool room temperature, or in the fridge, for 30 minutes.

4 Remove the monkfish from the marinade and broil for 10–12 minutes, turning once and brushing regularly with the marinade until cooked through.

5 Serve the monkfish garnished with coriander sprigs and lime slices and accompanied by the salsa.

COOK'S TIP
It is important to remove the tough pinkish-grey membrane covering the monkfish tail before cooking, otherwise it will shrink and toughen the monkfish.

Herrings with Walnut Stuffing

Ask the fishmonger to prepare the fish – mackerel can be used if herrings are not available.

Ingredients

Serves 4
2 tbsp butter
1 onion, finely chopped
6 tbsp fresh white bread crumbs
½ cup shelled walnuts, toasted
   and chopped
finely grated rind of ½ lemon
1 tbsp lemon juice
2 tsp whole grain mustard
3 tbsp mixed chopped fresh herbs, such
   as sage, thyme and parsley
4 herrings, about 10oz each, without
   heads and tails, boned
salt and black pepper
lemon wedges and flat leaf parsley
   sprigs, to garnish

1 Preheat the oven to 375°F. Melt the butter in a frying pan and gently fry the onion for about 10 minutes until golden.

2 Stir in the bread crumbs, chopped walnuts, lemon rind and juice, mustard and herbs. Mix together, then season with salt and pepper to taste.

3 Open out the herring fillets and divide the stuffing among them. Fold the herrings back in half and slash the skin several times on each side.

4 Arrange the herrings in a lightly greased shallow baking pan and bake for 20–25 minutes. Serve hot, garnished with lemon wedges and parsley sprigs.

Trout with Mushroom Sauce

Ingredients

Serves 4
8 trout fillets
seasoned flour
6 tbsp butter
1 garlic clove, chopped
2 tsp chopped fresh sage
12oz mixed wild or cultivated
   mushrooms
6 tbsp dry white wine
1 cup heavy cream
salt and black pepper
fresh sage sprigs, to garnish

Cook's Tip
Use a large sharp knife to ease the skin from the trout fillets, then pull out any bones from the flesh – a pair of tweezers makes easy work of this fiddly task!

1 Remove the skin from the trout fillets, then carefully remove any bones.

2 Lightly dust the trout fillets on both sides in the seasoned flour, shaking off any excess.

3 Melt the butter in a large frying pan, add the trout fillets and fry gently over a moderate heat for 4–5 minutes, turning once. Remove from the pan and keep warm.

4 Add the garlic, sage and mushrooms to the pan and fry until softened.

5 Pour in the wine and boil briskly to allow the alcohol to evaporate. Stir in the cream and seasoning.

6 Serve the trout fillets on warmed plates with the sauce spooned over. Garnish with a few fresh sage sprigs, if you like.

SPANISH-STYLE HAKE

Cod and haddock cutlets will work just as well as hake in this tasty fish dish.

INGREDIENTS

Serves 4
2 tbsp olive oil
2 tbsp butter
1 onion, chopped
3 garlic cloves, crushed
1 tbsp flour
½ tsp paprika
4 hake steaks, about 6oz each
8oz fine green beans, cut into
  1in lengths
1½ cups fresh fish stock
⅔ cup dry white wine
2 tbsp dry sherry
16–20 live mussels, cleaned
3 tbsp chopped fresh parsley
salt and black pepper
crusty bread, to serve

1 Heat the oil and butter in a sauté or frying pan, add the onion and cook for 5 minutes, until softened, but not browned. Add the crushed garlic and cook for 1 minute more.

2 Mix together the flour and paprika, then lightly dust over the hake steaks. Push the onion and garlic over to one side of the pan.

3 Add the hake steaks to the pan and fry until golden on both sides. Stir in the beans, stock, wine, sherry and seasoning. Bring to a boil and cook for about 2 minutes.

4 Add the mussels and parsley, cover the pan and cook for 5–8 minutes, until the mussels have opened.

5 Serve the hake in warmed, shallow soup bowls with plenty of crusty bread to mop up the juices.

GOLDEN FISH PIE

INGREDIENTS

Serves 4–6

1½lb white fish fillets
1¼ cups milk
flavoring ingredients (onion slices,
    bay leaf and black peppercorns)
4oz cooked, peeled shrimp, defrosted
    if frozen
½ cup butter
½ cup flour
1¼ cups light cream
3oz Gruyère cheese, grated
1 bunch watercress, leaves only, chopped
1 tsp Dijon mustard
5 sheets filo pastry
salt and black pepper

1 Place the fish fillets in a pan, pour over the milk and add the flavoring ingredients. Bring just to a boil, then cover and simmer for 10–12 minutes, until the fish is almost tender.

2 Skin and bone the fish, then roughly flake into a shallow ovenproof dish. Scatter the shrimp over the fish. Strain the milk and reserve.

3 Melt 4 tbsp of the butter in a pan. Stir in the flour and cook for 1 minute. Stir in the reserved milk and cream. Bring to a boil, stirring, then simmer for 2–3 minutes, until the sauce has thickened.

4 Remove the pan from the heat and stir in the Gruyère, watercress, mustard and seasoning to taste. Pour over the fish and leave to cool.

5 Preheat the oven to 375°F. Melt the remaining butter. Brush one sheet of filo pastry with a little butter, then crumple up loosely and place on top of the filling. Repeat this procedure with the remaining filo sheets and butter until they are all used up and the pie is completely covered.

6 Bake in the oven for 25–30 minutes, until the pastry is golden and crisp.

ROOT VEGETABLE COUSCOUS

Cheap and plentiful, autumn's crop of flavorful root vegetables is perfect for this delicious vegetarian main course. The spiced red sauce is fairly fiery and is not for the faint hearted! If you prefer your food less hot, leave out the harissa.

INGREDIENTS

Serves 4

2 cups couscous
3 tbsp olive oil
4 pearl onions, halved
1½lb mixed root vegetables, such as parsnips, carrots, rutabagas, turnip, celeriac and sweet potatoes, cut into chunks
2 garlic cloves, crushed
pinch of saffron strands
½ tsp ground cinnamon
½ tsp ground ginger
½ tsp ground turmeric
1 tsp ground cumin
1 tsp ground coriander
1 tbsp tomato paste
1⅞ cups hot vegetable stock
1 small fennel bulb, quartered
1 cup cooked or canned chick-peas
⅓ cup seedless raisins
2 tbsp chopped fresh coriander
2 tbsp chopped fresh flat leaf parsley
salt and black pepper

For the spiced red sauce
1 tbsp olive oil
1 tbsp lemon juice
1 tbsp chopped fresh coriander
½–1 tsp harissa

1 Put the couscous in a bowl, cover with hot water and drain. Spread out on to a tray and leave for about 20 minutes, sprinkling over a little water every 5 minutes to keep the couscous grains moist.

2 Meanwhile, heat the oil in a large frying pan and fry the onions for about 3 minutes. Add the mixed root vegetables and fry gently for about 5 minutes, until softened.

3 Add the garlic and spices to the frying pan and cook for 1 minute, stirring. Transfer the vegetable mixture to a large deep saucepan.

4 Stir the tomato paste and stock into the vegetable mixture, then add the fennel, chick-peas, raisins, chopped fresh coriander and flat leaf parsley. Bring to a boil.

5 Fork the couscous to break up any lumps and put into a steamer lined with cheesecloth and place the steamer over the vegetable mixture.

6 Cover the steamer with a lid or foil and simmer for 15–20 minutes, until the vegetables are tender and the couscous is piping hot.

7 To make the spiced red sauce, strain about 1 cup of the liquid from the vegetables into a small pan. Stir in the olive oil, lemon juice and coriander, and add harissa to taste.

8 Spoon the couscous on to a serving plate and pile the vegetables on top. Serve at once, handing round the spiced red sauce separately.

COOK'S TIP
Harissa is a very fiery Tunisian chili sauce. It can be bought ready-made in small cans from Middle-Eastern shops.

Corn and Bean Tamale Pie

Ingredients

Serves 4

2 ears of fresh corn
2 tbsp vegetable oil
1 onion, chopped
2 garlic cloves, crushed
1 red bell pepper, seeded and chopped
2 green chilies, seeded and chopped
2 tsp ground cumin
1lb ripe tomatoes, peeled, seeded and chopped
1 tbsp tomato paste
15oz can red kidney beans, drained and rinsed
1 tbsp chopped fresh oregano
oregano leaves, to garnish

For the topping

1 cup polenta
1 tbsp flour
½ tsp salt
2 tsp baking powder
1 egg, lightly beaten
½ cup milk
1 tbsp butter, melted
2oz smoked Cheddar cheese, grated

1 Preheat the oven to 425°F. Remove the outer husks and silky threads from the ears of corn, then parboil in boiling, but not salted, water for 8 minutes. Drain and leave until cool enough to handle, then run a sharp knife down the ears of corn to remove the kernels.

2 Heat the oil in a large pan and fry the onion, garlic and pepper for 5 minutes, until softened. Add the chilies and cumin and fry for 1 minute.

3 Stir in the tomatoes, tomato paste, beans, corn kernels and oregano. Season. Bring to a boil, then simmer, uncovered, for 10 minutes.

4 Meanwhile, make the topping. Mix together the polenta, flour, salt, baking powder, egg, milk and butter in a bowl to form a smooth, thick batter.

5 Transfer the corn kernels and beans to an ovenproof dish, spoon the polenta mixture over the top and spread evenly. Bake for 30 minutes. Remove from the oven, sprinkle over the cheese, then return to the oven for a further 5–10 minutes, until golden.

BEANS WITH MUSHROOMS

A mixture of wild and cultivated mushrooms helps to give this dish a rich and nutty flavor.

INGREDIENTS

Serves 4
2 *tbsp olive oil*
4 *tbsp butter*
2 *shallots, chopped*
2–3 *garlic cloves, crushed*
1½*lb mixed mushrooms, thickly sliced*
4 *pieces sun-dried tomatoes in oil,*
   drained and chopped
6 *tbsp dry white wine*
15*oz can red kidney, pinto or borlotti*
   beans, drained
3 *tbsp grated Parmesan cheese*
2 *tbsp chopped fresh parsley*
salt and black pepper
freshly cooked pappardelle *pasta,*
   to serve

1 Heat the oil and butter in a frying pan and fry the shallots until soft.

2 Add the garlic and mushrooms to the pan and fry for 3–4 minutes. Stir in the sun-dried tomatoes, wine and seasoning to taste.

3 Stir in the beans and cook for about 5–6 minutes, until most of the liquid has evaporated and the beans are warmed through.

4 Stir in the grated Parmesan cheese. Sprinkle with parsley and serve immediately with *pappardelle*.

PEAR AND ROQUEFORT SALAD

Choose ripe, firm Comice or Bartlett pears for this salad.

INGREDIENTS

Serves 4
3 ripe pears
lemon juice
about 6oz mixed salad leaves
6oz Roquefort cheese
½ cup hazelnut kernels, toasted
*   and chopped*

For the dressing
2 tbsp hazelnut oil
3 tbsp olive oil
1 tbsp cider vinegar
1 tsp Dijon mustard
salt and black pepper

1 To make the dressing, mix together the oils, vinegar and mustard in a bowl or screw-topped jar. Add salt and black pepper to taste.

2 Peel, core and slice the pears and toss them in lemon juice.

3 Arrange the salad leaves on serving plates, then place the pears on top. Crumble the cheese and scatter over the salad with the hazelnuts. Spoon over the dressing and serve at once.

ONION AND GRUYÈRE TART

The secret of this tart is to cook the onions very slowly until they almost caramelize.

INGREDIENTS

Serves 4
1½ cups flour
pinch of salt
6 tbsp butter, diced
1 egg yolk

For the filling
4 tbsp butter
1lb onions, thinly sliced
1–2 tbsp whole grain mustard
2 eggs, plus 1 egg yolk
1 cup heavy cream
3oz Gruyère cheese, grated
freshly grated nutmeg
salt and black pepper

1 To make the pastry, sift the flour and salt into a bowl, then rub in the butter until the mixture resembles fine breadcrumbs. Add the egg yolk and 1 tbsp cold water and mix to a firm dough. Chill for 30 minutes.

2 Preheat the oven to 400°F. Knead the pastry, then roll out on a floured board and use to line a 9in pie pan. Prick the base with a fork, line the pastry crust with wax paper and fill with baking beans.

3 Bake the pastry crust for 15 minutes. Remove the paper and beans and bake for a further 10–15 minutes, until the pastry crust is crisp. Meanwhile, melt the butter and cook the onions in a covered pan for 20 minutes, stirring occasionally, until golden.

4 Reduce the oven temperature to 350°F. Spread the base with mustard and top with the onions. Mix together the eggs, egg yolk, cream, cheese, nutmeg and seasoning. Pour over the onions. Bake for 30–35 minutes, until golden. Serve warm.

Baked Squash with Parmesan

Spaghetti squash is an unusual vegetable – the flesh separates into long strands when baked. One squash makes an excellent supper dish for two.

Ingredients

Serves 2

1 medium spaghetti squash
½ cup butter
3 tbsp chopped mixed fresh herbs, such as parsley, chives and oregano
1 garlic clove, crushed
1 shallot, chopped
1 tsp lemon juice
½ cup freshly grated Parmesan cheese
salt and black pepper

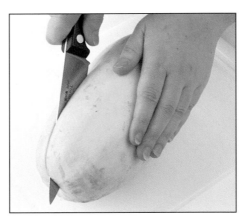

1 Preheat the oven to 350°F. Cut the squash in half lengthwise. Place the halves, cut side down, in a roasting pan. Pour a little water around them, and then bake for about 40 minutes, until tender.

2 Meanwhile, put the butter, herbs, garlic, shallot and lemon juice in a food processor and process until thoroughly blended and creamy in consistency. Season to taste.

3 When the squash is tender, scrape out any seeds and cut a thin slice from the base of each half, so that they will sit level. Place the squash halves on warmed serving plates.

4 Using a fork, pull out a few of the spaghetti-like strands in the center of each. Add a dollop of herb butter, then sprinkle with a little of the grated Parmesan. Serve the remaining herb butter and Parmesan separately, adding them as you pull out more strands.

POTATO CAKES WITH GOAT CHEESE

INGREDIENTS

Serves 2–4

1lb potatoes
2 tsp chopped fresh thyme
1 garlic clove, crushed
2 scallions (including the green parts),
   finely chopped
2 tbsp olive oil
4 tbsp unsalted butter
2½oz Crottins de Chavignol (firm goat
   cheeses)
salt and black pepper
salad leaves, such as chicory, radicchio
   and lamb's lettuce, tossed in walnut
   dressing, to serve
thyme sprigs, to garnish

1 Peel and coarsely grate the potatoes. Using your hands squeeze out all the excess moisture, then carefully combine with the chopped thyme, garlic, scallions and seasoning.

2 Heat half the oil and butter in a non-stick frying pan. Add two large spoonfuls of the potato mixture, spacing them well apart, and press firmly down with a spatula. Cook for 3–4 minutes on each side until golden.

3 Drain the potato cakes on paper towels and keep warm in a low oven. Make two more potato cakes in the same way with the remaining mixture. Meanwhile, preheat the broiler.

4 Cut the cheese in half horizontally and place one half, cut side up, on each potato cake. Broil for 2–3 minutes until golden. Transfer the potato cakes to serving plates and arrange the salad leaves around them. Garnish with thyme sprigs and serve at once.

PLUM AND PORT MOUSSE

INGREDIENTS

Serves 6
1lb ripe red plums
3 tbsp granulated sugar
4 tbsp ruby port
1 tbsp/1 package powdered
  gelatin
3 eggs, separated
½ cup superfine sugar
⅔ cup heavy cream
skinned and chopped pistachio nuts,
  to decorate
cinnamon cookies, to serve (optional)

1 Place the plums and granulated sugar in a pan with 2 tbsp water. Cook over a low heat until softened. Press the fruit through a sieve to remove the pits and skins. Leave to cool, then stir in the port.

2 Put 3 tbsp water in a small bowl, sprinkle over the gelatin and leave to soften. Stand the bowl in a pan of hot water and leave until dissolved. Stir into the plum purée.

3 Place the egg yolks and superfine sugar in a bowl and whisk until thick and mousse-like. Fold in the plum purée, then whip the cream and fold in gently.

4 Whisk the egg whites until holding stiff peaks, then carefully fold in using a metal spoon. Divide among six glasses and chill until set.

5 Decorate the mousses with chopped pistachio nuts and serve with crisp cinnamon cookies, if liked.

> COOK'S TIP
> If you would prefer a non-alcoholic mousse, use red grape juice in place of the port.

WARM AUTUMN COMPÔTE

A simple yet quite sophisticated dessert featuring succulent, ripe autumnal fruits.

INGREDIENTS

Serves 4
6 tbsp sugar
1 bottle red wine
1 vanilla pod, split
1 strip pared lemon rind
4 pears
2 purple figs, quartered
8oz raspberries
lemon juice, to taste

1 Put the sugar and wine in a large pan and heat gently until dissolved. Add the vanilla pod and lemon rind and bring to a boil. Simmer for 5 minutes.

2 Peel and halve the pears, then scoop out the cores, using a melon baller. Add the pears to the syrup and poach for 15 minutes, turning the pears several times so they color evenly.

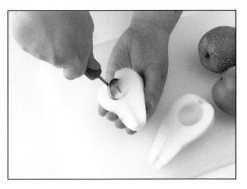

3 Add the figs and poach for a further 5 minutes, until the fruits are tender.

4 Transfer the poached pears and figs to a serving bowl using a slotted spoon, then scatter over the raspberries.

5 Return the syrup to the heat and boil rapidly to reduce slightly and concentrate the flavor. Add a little lemon juice to taste. Strain the syrup over the fruits and serve warm.

Iced Chocolate and Nut Gâteau

Autumn hazelnuts add crunchiness to this delicious iced dessert.

Ingredients

Serves 6–8

½ cup shelled hazelnuts
about 32 ladyfingers
⅔ cup cold strong black coffee
2 tbsp brandy
1⅞ cups heavy cream
6 tbsp confectioners' sugar, sifted
5oz semisweet chocolate
confectioners' sugar and cocoa, for
    dusting

1 Preheat the oven to 400°F. Spread out the hazelnuts on a baking sheet and toast them in the oven for about 5 minutes until golden.

2 Transfer the nuts to a clean dish towel and rub off the skins while still warm. Cool, then chop finely.

3 Line a 2 pint/5 cup loaf pan with plastic wrap and cut the ladyfingers to fit the base and sides. Reserve the remaining ladyfingers.

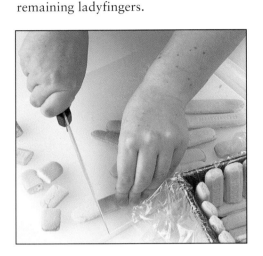

4 Mix the coffee with the brandy in a shallow dish. Dip the ladyfingers briefly into the coffee mixture and return to the pan, sugary side down.

5 Whip the cream with the confectioners' sugar until it holds soft peaks. Roughly chop 3oz of the chocolate, and fold into the cream with the hazelnuts.

6 Melt the remaining chocolate in a bowl set over a pan of barely simmering water. Cool, then fold into the cream mixture. Spoon into the pan.

7 Moisten the remaining ladyfingers in the coffee mixture and lay over the filling. Wrap and freeze until firm.

8 To serve, remove from the freezer 30 minutes before serving. Turn out on to a serving plate and dust with confectioners' sugar and cocoa.

BLACKBERRY BROWN SUGAR MERINGUE

INGREDIENTS

Serves 6
1 cup light brown sugar
3 egg whites
1 tsp distilled malt vinegar
½ tsp vanilla extract

For the filling
12oz–1lb blackberries
2 tbsp black currant liqueur
1¼ cups heavy cream
1 tbsp confectioners' sugar, sifted
blackberry leaves, to decorate
(optional)

1 Preheat the oven to 325°F. Draw an 8in circle on a sheet of wax paper, then turn it over and place on a baking sheet.

2 Spread out the brown sugar on a baking sheet and dry in the oven for 8–10 minutes. Sieve to remove lumps.

3 Whisk the egg whites in a bowl until stiff. Add half the dried brown sugar, 1 tbsp at a time, whisking well after each addition. Add the vinegar and vanilla extract, then fold in the remaining sugar.

4 Spoon the meringue on to the drawn circle on the paper, leaving a hollow in the center. Bake for 45 minutes, then turn off the oven and leave the meringue in the oven with the door slightly open, until cold.

5 Place the blackberries in a bowl, sprinkle over the liqueur and leave to macerate for 30 minutes.

6 When the meringue is cold, carefully peel off the wax paper and transfer the meringue to a serving plate. Lightly whip the cream with the confectioners' sugar and spoon into the center. Top with the blackberries and decorate with small blackberry leaves, if liked. Serve the meringue at once.

PEAR AND BLUEBERRY PIE

INGREDIENTS

Serves 4
2 cups flour
pinch of salt
4 tbsp lard, cubed
4 tbsp butter, cubed
1½lb blueberries
2 tbsp sugar
1 tbsp arrowroot
2 ripe, but firm pears, peeled, cored
   and sliced
½ tsp ground cinnamon
grated rind of ½ lemon
beaten egg, to glaze
sugar, for sprinkling
crème fraîche or heavy cream, to serve

1 Sift the flour and salt into a bowl and rub in the lard and butter until the mixture resembles fine breadcrumbs. Stir in 3 tbsp cold water and mix to a dough. Chill for 30 minutes.

2 Place 8oz of the blueberries in a pan with the sugar. Cover and cook gently until the blueberries have softened. Press through a nylon sieve.

3 Blend the arrowroot with 2 tbsp cold water and add to the blueberry purée. Bring to a boil, stirring until thickened. Cool slightly.

4 Place a baking sheet in the oven and preheat to 375°F. Roll out just over half the pastry on a lightly floured surface and use to line an 8in shallow pie pan.

5 Mix together the remaining blueberries, the pears, cinnamon and lemon rind and spoon into the dish. Pour over the blueberry purée.

6 Roll out the remaining pastry and use to cover the pie. Make a small slit in the center. Brush with beaten egg and sprinkle with sugar. Bake the pie on the hot baking sheet, for 40–45 minutes, until golden. Serve warm with crème fraîche or heavy cream.

APPLE SOUFFLÉ OMELETTE

Apples sautéed until they are slightly caramelized make a delicious autumn filling – you could use fresh raspberries or strawberries in the summer.

INGREDIENTS

Serves 2
4 eggs, separated
2 tbsp light cream
1 tbsp sugar
1 tbsp butter
confectioners' sugar, for dredging

For the filling
1 apple, peeled, cored and sliced
2 tbsp butter
2 tbsp light brown sugar
3 tbsp light cream

1 To make the filling, sauté the apple slices in the butter and sugar until just tender. Stir in the cream and keep warm, while making the omelette.

2 Place the egg yolks in a bowl with the cream and sugar and beat well. Whisk the egg whites until stiff, then fold into the yolk mixture.

3 Melt the butter in a large heavy-based frying pan, pour in the soufflé mixture and spread evenly. Cook for 1 minute until golden underneath, then place under a hot broiler to brown the top.

4 Slide the omelette on to a plate, add the apple mixture, then fold over. Sift the confectioners' sugar over thickly, then mark in a criss-cross pattern with a hot metal skewer. Serve immediately.

WINTER

Winter is the time for warm and nourishing foods. It is a good time for root vegetables, essential for soups and casseroles, and potatoes for baking. Nuts are plentiful, especially chestnuts and walnuts, which lend themselves to a variety of dishes, such as Nut Patties with Mango Relish, and Chocolate and Chestnut Roulade. Make good use of imported citrus fruits in desserts like Clementines in Cinnamon Caramel, and Tangerine Yogurt Ice. The shops will certainly have a new season's supply of dried dates and figs, which are delicious at the end of a meal with nuts or in a dessert like Chocolate Date Torte. There are still supplies of game, so make use of it before the season draws to a close. Excellent white fish is available, particularly cod and haddock, and also seasonal mussels and scallops. Introduce new tastes with smoked fish in dishes such as Smoked Trout Pilaf and Seafood Pancakes.

JERUSALEM ARTICHOKE SOUP

Topped with saffron cream, this soup is wonderful on a chilly day.

Serves 4
4 tbsp butter
1 onion, chopped
1lb Jerusalem artichokes, peeled and cut into chunks
3¾ cups chicken stock
⅔ cup milk
⅔ cup heavy cream
good pinch of saffron powder
salt and black pepper
snipped fresh chives, to garnish

1 Melt the butter in a large heavy-based pan and cook the onion for 5–8 minutes, until soft but not browned, stirring occasionally.

2 Add the artichokes to the pan and stir until coated in the butter. Cover and cook gently for 10–15 minutes; do not allow the artichokes to brown. Pour in the stock and milk, then cover and simmer for 15 minutes. Cool slightly, then process in a blender or food processor until smooth.

3 Strain the soup back into the pan. Add half the cream, season to taste, and reheat gently. Lightly whip the remaining cream and saffron powder. Ladle the soup into warmed soup bowls and put a spoonful of saffron cream in the center of each. Scatter over the snipped chives and serve at once.

BROCCOLI AND STILTON SOUP

A really easy, but rich, soup – choose something simple to follow, such as plainly roasted or broiled meat, poultry or fish.

Serves 4
12oz broccoli
2 tbsp butter
1 onion, chopped
1 leek, white part only, chopped
1 small potato, cut into chunks
2½ cups hot chicken stock
1¼ cups milk
3 tbsp heavy cream
4oz Stilton cheese, rind removed, crumbled
salt and black pepper

1 Break the broccoli into florets, discarding tough stems. Set aside two small florets for the garnish.

2 Melt the butter in a large pan and cook the onion and leek until soft but not colored. Add the broccoli and potato, then pour in the stock. Cover and simmer for 15–20 minutes, until the vegetables are tender.

3 Cool slightly, then purée in a blender or food processor. Strain through a sieve back into the pan.

4 Add the milk, cream and seasoning to the pan and reheat gently. At the last minute add the cheese, stirring until it just melts. Do not boil.

5 Meanwhile, blanch the reserved broccoli florets and cut them vertically into thin slices. Ladle the soup into warmed bowls and garnish with the broccoli florets and a generous grinding of black pepper.

CHICKEN LIVER PÂTÉ WITH MARSALA

This is a really quick and simple pâté to make, yet it has a delicious – and quite sophisticated – flavor. It contains Marsala, a soft and pungent fortified wine from Sicily. If it is unavailable, use brandy or a medium-dry sherry.

INGREDIENTS

Serves 4

12oz chicken livers, defrosted
 if frozen
1 cup butter, softened
2 garlic cloves, crushed
1 tbsp Marsala
1 tsp chopped fresh sage
salt and black pepper
8 sage leaves, to garnish
Melba toast, to serve

1 Pick over the chicken livers, then rinse and dry with kitchen paper. Melt 2 tbsp of the butter in a frying pan, and fry the chicken livers with the garlic over a medium heat for about 5 minutes, or until they are firm but still pink in the middle.

2 Transfer the livers to a blender or food processor, using a slotted spoon, and add the Marsala and chopped sage.

3 Melt 10 tbsp of the remaining butter in the frying pan, stirring to loosen any sediment, then pour into the blender or processor and blend until smooth. Season well.

4 Spoon the pâté into four individual pots and smooth the surface. Melt the remaining butter in a separate pan and pour over the pâtés. Garnish with sage leaves and chill until set. Serve with triangles of Melba toast.

SALMON RILLETTES

──────── INGREDIENTS ────────

Serves 6
12oz salmon fillets
¾ cup butter, softened
1 celery stalk, finely chopped
1 leek, white part only, finely chopped
1 bay leaf
⅔ cup dry white wine
4oz smoked salmon trimmings
generous pinch of ground mace
4 tbsp ricotta
salt and black pepper
salad leaves, to serve

1 Lightly season the salmon. Melt 2 tbsp of the butter in a medium sauté pan. Add the celery and leek and cook for about 5 minutes. Add the salmon and bay leaf and pour over the wine. Cover and cook for about 15 minutes until the fish is tender.

2 Strain the cooking liquid into a pan and boil until reduced to about 2 tbsp. Cool. Meanwhile, melt 4 tbsp of the remaining butter and gently cook the smoked salmon until it turns pale pink. Leave to cool.

3 Remove the skin and any bones from the salmon fillets. Flake the flesh into a bowl and add the reduced, cooled cooking liquid.

4 Beat in the remaining butter, the mace and ricotta. Break up the smoked salmon trimmings and fold into the mixture with the pan juices. Taste and adjust the seasoning.

5 Spoon the salmon mixture into a dish or terrine and smooth the top level. Cover and chill for up to 2 days.

6 To serve the salmon rillettes, shape the mixture into oval quenelles using two dessert spoons and arrange on individual plates with the salad leaves. Accompany with brown bread or wheat crackers, if you like.

MELON AND GRAPEFRUIT COCKTAIL

This pretty, colorful starter can be made in minutes, so it is perfect for when you don't have time to cook, but want something really special to eat.

INGREDIENTS

Serves 4
1 small Ogen melon
1 small Charentais melon
2 pink grapefruit
3 tbsp orange juice
4 tbsp red vermouth
seeds from ½ pomegranate
mint sprigs, to decorate

COOK'S TIP
To check if the melons are ripe, smell them – they should have a heady aroma, and give slightly when pressed at the stalk end.

---

1 Halve the melons lengthwise and scoop out all the seeds. Cut into wedges and remove the skins, then cut across into large bite-sized pieces.

2 Using a small sharp knife, cut the peel and pith from the grapefruit. Holding the fruit over a bowl to catch the juice, cut between the grapefruit membranes to release the segments. Set aside the grapefruit segments.

3 Stir the orange juice and vermouth into the reserved grapefruit juice.

4 Arrange the melon pieces and grapefruit segments haphazardly on four individual serving plates. Spoon over the dressing, then scatter with the pomegranate seeds. Decorate with mint sprigs and serve at once.

PROSCIUTTO WITH MANGO

Other fresh, colorful fruits, such as figs, papaya or melon would go equally well with the prosciutto in this light, elegant starter. It is amazingly simple to prepare and can be made in advance – ideal if you are serving a complicated main course.

INGREDIENTS

Serves 4
16 slices prosciutto
1 ripe mango
black pepper
flat leaf parsley sprigs, to garnish

1 Separate the prosciutto slices and arrange four on each of four individual plates, crumpling the meat slightly to give a decorative effect.

2 Cut the mango into three thick slices around the pit, then slice the flesh and discard the pit. Neatly cut away the skin from each slice.

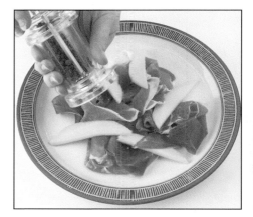

3 Arrange the mango slices in among the prosciutto. Grind over some black pepper and serve garnished with flat leaf parsley sprigs.

CELERIAC FRITTERS WITH MUSTARD DIP

The combination of the hot, crispy fritters and cold mustard dip is extremely good.

INGREDIENTS

Serves 4

1 egg
1½ cups ground almonds
3 tbsp freshly grated Parmesan cheese
3 tbsp chopped fresh parsley
1 medium celeriac, about 1lb
lemon juice
oil, for deep-frying
⅔ cup sour cream
1–2 tbsp whole grain mustard
salt and black pepper
sea salt flakes, for sprinkling

1 Beat the egg well and pour into a shallow dish. Mix together the almonds, grated Parmesan and parsley in a separate dish. Season with salt and plenty of pepper. Set aside.

2 Peel and cut the celeriac into strips about ½in wide and 2in long. Drop them immediately into a bowl of water with a little lemon juice added to prevent discoloration.

3 Heat the oil to 350°F. Drain and then pat dry half the celeriac chips. Dip them into the beaten egg, then into the ground almond mixture, making sure that the pieces are coated completely and evenly.

4 Deep-fry the celeriac fritters, a few at a time, for 2–3 minutes until golden. Drain on paper towels and keep warm while you cook the remainder.

5 Meanwhile, to make the mustard dip, mix together the sour cream, mustard and salt to taste. Spoon into a small serving bowl.

6 Heap the celeriac fritters on to warmed serving plates. Sprinkle with sea salt flakes and serve at once with the mustard dip.

GRILLED GARLIC MUSSELS

——— INGREDIENTS ———

Serves 4
3 – 3½lb live mussels
½ cup dry white wine
4 tbsp butter
2 shallots, finely chopped
2 garlic cloves, crushed
6 tbsp dried white
  bread crumbs
4 tbsp chopped fresh mixed herbs,
  such as flat leaf parsley, basil and
  oregano
2 tbsp freshly grated Parmesan
  cheese
salt and black pepper
basil leaves, to garnish

1 Scrub the mussels well under cold running water. Remove the beards and discard any mussels that are open.

2 Place the mussels in a large pan with the wine. Cover the pan and cook over a high heat, shaking the pan occasionally for 5 – 8 minutes, until the mussels have opened.

4 Allow the mussels to cool slightly, then remove and discard the top half of each shell, leaving the mussels on the remaining halves.

5 Melt the butter in a pan and fry the shallots until softened. Add the garlic and cook for 1 – 2 minutes.

3 Strain the mussels and reserve the cooking liquid. Discard any mussels that still remain closed.

6 Stir in the bread crumbs and cook, stirring until lightly browned. Remove the pan from the heat and stir in the herbs. Moisten with a little of the reserved mussel liquid, then season to taste with salt and pepper.

7 Spoon the bread crumb mixture over the mussels in their shells and arrange on baking sheets. Sprinkle with the grated Parmesan.

8 Cook the mussels under a hot broiler in batches for about 2 minutes, until the topping is crisp and golden. Keep the cooked mussels warm in a low oven while broiling the remainder. Garnish with basil leaves and serve hot.

VENISON WITH CRANBERRY SAUCE

Venison steaks are now readily available. Lean and low in fat, they make a healthy choice for a special occasion. Served with a sauce of fresh seasonal cranberries, port and ginger, they make a dish with a wonderful combination of flavors.

INGREDIENTS

Serves 4

1 orange
1 lemon
1 cup fresh or frozen cranberries, picked over
1 tsp grated fresh ginger root
1 thyme sprig
1 tsp Dijon mustard
4 tbsp red currant jelly
⅔ cup ruby port
2 tbsp sunflower oil
4 venison steaks
2 shallots, finely chopped
salt and black pepper
thyme sprigs, to garnish
creamy mashed potatoes and broccoli, to serve

1 Pare the rind from half the orange and half the lemon using a vegetable peeler, then cut into very fine strips.

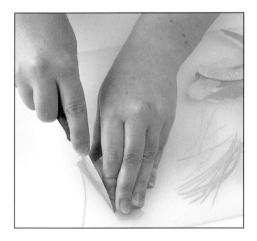

2 Blanch the strips in a small pan of boiling water for about 5 minutes until tender. Drain the strips and refresh under cold water.

3 Squeeze the juice from the orange and lemon and then pour into a small pan. Add the fresh or frozen cranberries, ginger, thyme sprig, mustard, red currant jelly and port. Cook over a low heat until the jelly melts.

4 Bring the sauce to a boil, stirring occasionally, then cover the pan and reduce the heat. Cook gently, for about 15 minutes, until the cranberries are just tender.

5 Heat the oil in a heavy-based frying pan, add the venison steaks and cook over a high heat for 2–3 minutes.

6 Turn over the steaks and add the shallots to the pan. Cook the steaks on the other side for 2–3 minutes, depending on whether you like rare or medium cooked meat.

7 Just before the end of cooking, pour in the sauce and add the strips of orange and lemon rind.

8 Leave the sauce to bubble for a few seconds to thicken slightly, then remove the thyme sprig and adjust the seasoning to taste.

9 Transfer the venison steaks to warmed plates and spoon over the sauce. Garnish with thyme sprigs and serve accompanied by creamy mashed potatoes and broccoli.

COOK'S TIP
When frying venison, always remember the briefer the better; venison will turn to leather if subjected to fierce heat after it has reached the medium-rare stage. If you dislike any hint of pink, cook it to this stage then let it rest in a low oven for a few minutes.

VARIATION
When fresh cranberries are unavailable, use red currants instead. Stir them into the sauce towards the end of cooking with the orange and lemon rinds.

Rich Beef Casserole

Serves 4–6

2lb chuck steak, cut into cubes
2 onions, coarsely chopped
1 bouquet garni
6 black peppercorns
1 tbsp red wine vinegar
1 bottle full-bodied red wine
3–4 tbsp olive oil
3 celery stalks, thickly sliced
½ cup flour
1¼ cups beef stock
2 tbsp tomato paste
2 garlic cloves, crushed
6oz cremini mushrooms,
*   halved*
14oz can artichoke hearts, drained and
*   halved*
chopped fresh parsley and thyme,
*   to garnish*
creamy mashed potatoes, to serve

1 Place the meat in a bowl. Add the onions, bouquet garni, peppercorns, vinegar and wine. Stir well, cover and leave to marinate overnight.

2 The next day, preheat the oven to 325°F. Strain the meat, reserving the marinade. Pat the meat dry with paper towels.

3 Heat the oil in a large flameproof casserole and fry the meat and onions in batches, adding a little more oil, if necessary. Remove and set aside.

4 Add the celery to the casserole and fry until lightly browned. Remove and set aside with the meat and onions.

5 Sprinkle the flour into the casserole and cook for 1 minute. Gradually add the reserved marinade and the stock, and bring to a boil, stirring. Return the meat, onions and celery to the casserole, then stir in the tomato paste and crushed garlic.

6 Cover the casserole and cook in the oven for about 2¼ hours. Stir in the mushrooms and artichokes, cover again and cook for a further 15 minutes, until the meat is tender. Garnish with chopped parsley and thyme, and serve hot with creamy mashed potatoes.

PORK STEAKS WITH GREMOLATA

Gremolata is a popular Italian dressing of garlic, lemon and parsley – it adds a hint of sharpness to the pork.

INGREDIENTS

Serves 4
2 tbsp olive oil
4 pork shoulder steaks
1 onion, chopped
2 garlic cloves, crushed
2 tbsp tomato paste
14oz can chopped tomatoes
⅔ cup dry white wine
bouquet garni
3 anchovy fillets, drained and chopped
salt and black pepper
salad leaves, to serve

For the gremolata
3 tbsp chopped fresh parsley
grated rind of ½ lemon
grated rind of 1 lime
1 garlic clove, chopped

1 Heat the oil in a large flameproof casserole, add the pork steaks and brown on both sides. Remove the steaks from the casserole.

2 Add the onion to the casserole and cook until soft and beginning to brown. Add the garlic and cook for 1–2 minutes, then stir in the tomato paste, chopped tomatoes and wine. Add the bouquet garni. Bring to a boil, then boil rapidly for 3–4 minutes to reduce and thicken slightly.

3 Return the pork to the casserole, then cover and cook for about 30 minutes. Stir in the chopped anchovies.

4 Cover the casserole and cook for a further 15 minutes, or until the pork is tender. Meanwhile, to make the gremolata, mix together the parsley, lemon and lime rinds and garlic.

5 Remove the pork steaks and discard the bouquet garni. Reduce the sauce over a high heat, if it is not already thick. Taste and adjust the seasoning.

6 Return the pork to the casserole, then sprinkle with the gremolata. Cover and cook for a further 5 minutes, then serve hot with salad leaves.

FIVE-SPICE LAMB

This aromatic lamb dish is perfect for an informal supper party.

INGREDIENTS

Serves 4

2–3 tbsp oil
3–3½lb leg of lamb, boned and cubed
1 onion, chopped
2 tsp grated fresh ginger root
1 garlic clove, crushed
1 tsp five-spice powder
2 tbsp hoisin sauce
1 tbsp light soy sauce
1¼ cups crushed tomatoes
1 cup lamb stock
1 red bell pepper, seeded and cubed
1 yellow bell pepper, seeded and cubed
2 tbsp chopped fresh coriander
1 tbsp sesame seeds, toasted
salt and black pepper

1 Preheat the oven to 325°F. Heat 2 tbsp of the oil in a flameproof casserole and then brown the lamb in batches over a high heat. Remove the meat and set aside.

2 Add the onion, ginger and garlic to the casserole with a little more of the oil, if necessary, and cook for about 5 minutes, until softened.

3 Return the lamb to the casserole. Stir in the five-spice powder, hoisin and soy sauces, crushed tomatoes, stock and seasoning. Bring to a boil, then cover and cook in the oven for 1¼ hours.

4 Remove the casserole from the oven, stir in the peppers, then cover and return to the oven for a further 15 minutes, or until the lamb is very tender.

5 Sprinkle with the coriander and sesame seeds. Serve hot.

STIR-FRIED TURKEY WITH SNOW PEAS

INGREDIENTS

Serves 4

2 tbsp sesame oil
6 tbsp lemon juice
1 garlic clove, crushed
½in piece fresh ginger root, peeled and
  grated
1 tsp honey
1lb turkey fillets, cut into strips
4oz snow peas, trimmed
2 tbsp groundnut oil
⅓ cup cashew nuts
6 scallions, cut into strips
8oz can water chestnuts, drained and
  thinly sliced
salt
saffron rice, to serve

1 Mix together the sesame oil, lemon juice, garlic, ginger and honey in a shallow non-metallic dish. Add the turkey and mix well. Cover and leave to marinate for 3–4 hours.

2 Blanch the snow peas in boiling salted water for 1 minute. Drain and refresh under cold running water.

3 Drain the marinade from the turkey strips and reserve the marinade. Heat the groundnut oil in a wok or large frying pan, add the cashew nuts and stir-fry for about 1–2 minutes until golden brown. Remove the cashew nuts from the wok or frying pan using a slotted spoon and set aside.

4 Add the turkey and stir-fry for 3–4 minutes, until golden brown. Add the scallions, snow peas, water chestnuts and the reserved marinade. Cook for a few minutes, until the turkey is tender and the sauce is bubbling and hot. Stir in the cashew nuts and serve with saffron rice.

CHICKEN, LEEK AND PARSLEY PIE

Serves 4–6

For the pastry
2½ cups flour
pinch of salt
⅞ cup butter, diced
2 egg yolks

For the filling
3 part-boned chicken breasts
flavoring ingredients (bouquet garni,
    black peppercorns, onion and carrot)
4 tbsp butter
2 leeks, thinly sliced
2oz Cheddar cheese, grated
1oz Parmesan cheese, finely grated
3 tbsp chopped fresh parsley
2 tbsp whole grain mustard
1 tsp cornstarch
1¼ cups heavy cream
salt and black pepper
beaten egg, to glaze
mixed green salad, to serve

1 To make the pastry, first sift the flour and salt. Blend together the butter and egg yolks in a food processor until creamy. Add the flour and process until the mixture is just coming together. Add about 1 tbsp cold water and process for a few seconds more. Turn out on to a lightly floured surface and knead lightly. Wrap in plastic wrap and chill for about 1 hour.

2 Meanwhile, poach the chicken breasts in water to cover, with the flavoring ingredients added, until tender. Leave to cool in the liquid.

3 Preheat the oven to 400°F. Divide the pastry into two pieces, one slightly larger than the other. Roll out the larger piece on a lightly floured surface and use to line a 7 x 11in baking dish or pan. Prick the base with a fork and bake for 15 minutes. Leave to cool.

4 Lift the cooled chicken from the poaching liquid and discard the skins and bones. Cut the chicken flesh into strips, then set aside.

5 Melt the butter in a frying pan and fry the leeks over a low heat, stirring occasionally, until soft.

6 Stir in the Cheddar, Parmesan and chopped parsley. Spread half the leek mixture over the cooked pastry base, leaving a border all the way around. Cover the leek mixture with the chicken strips, then top with the remaining leek mixture.

7 Mix together the mustard, cornstarch and cream in a small bowl. Add seasoning to taste. Pour over the filling.

8 Moisten the edges of the cooked pastry base. Roll out the remaining pastry and use to cover the pie. Brush with beaten egg and bake for 30–40 minutes until golden and crisp. Serve hot, cut into square portions, with a mixed green salad.

COOK'S TIP
This pastry is quite fragile and may break; the high fat content, however, means you can patch it together by pressing pieces of pastry trimmings into any cracks.

SEAFOOD CREPES

The combination of fresh and smoked haddock imparts a wonderful flavor to the filling.

INGREDIENTS

Serves 4–6
For the crepes
1 cup flour
pinch of salt
1 egg, plus 1 egg yolk
1¼ cups milk
1 tbsp melted butter, plus extra for cooking
2–3oz Gruyère cheese, grated

For the filling
8oz smoked haddock fillet
8oz fresh haddock fillet
1¼ cups milk
⅔ cup light cream
3 tbsp butter
4 tbsp flour
freshly grated nutmeg
2 hard-boiled eggs, shelled and chopped
salt and black pepper
curly salad leaves, to serve

1 To make the crepes, sift the flour and salt into a bowl. Make a well in the center and add the eggs. Whisk the eggs, starting to incorporate some of the flour from around the edges.

2 Gradually add the milk, whisking all the time until the batter is smooth and the consistency of thin cream. Stir in the melted butter.

3 Heat a small crepe pan or omelette pan until hot, then rub around the inside of the pan with a pad of paper towel dipped in melted butter.

4 Pour about 2 tbsp of the batter into the pan, then tip the pan to coat the base evenly. Cook for about 30 seconds until the underside of the crepe is brown.

5 Flip the crepe over and cook the other side until lightly browned. Repeat to make 12 crepes, rubbing the pan with melted butter between each crepe. Stack the crepes as you make them between sheets of wax paper. Keep warm on a plate set over a pan of simmering water.

6 Put the haddock fillets in a large pan. Add the milk and poach for 6–8 minutes, until just tender. Lift out the fish using a slotted spoon and, when cool enough to handle, remove the skin and any bones. Reserve the milk.

7 Measure the light cream into a measuring cup, then strain enough of the milk into the cup to make the quantity up to 1⅞ cups.

8 Melt the butter in a pan, stir in the flour and cook gently for 1 minute. Gradually mix in the milk mixture, stirring continuously to make a smooth sauce. Cook for 2–3 minutes, until thickened. Season with salt, pepper and nutmeg. Coarsely flake the haddock and fold into the sauce with the eggs. Leave to cool.

9 Preheat the oven to 350°F. Divide the filling among the crepes. Fold the sides of each crepe into the center, then roll them up to enclose the filling completely.

10 Butter four or six individual ovenproof dishes and arrange 2–3 filled crepes in each, or butter one large dish for all the crepes. Brush with melted butter and cook for 15 minutes. Sprinkle over the Gruyère and cook for a further 5 minutes, until warmed through. Serve hot with a few curly salad leaves.

VARIATION
For a different taste, add cooked, peeled shrimp, smoked mussels or cooked fresh, shelled mussels to the filling, instead of the chopped hard-boiled eggs.

CHILI SHRIMP

This delightful, spicy combination makes a lovely light main course for a casual supper. Serve with rice, noodles or freshly cooked pasta and a leafy salad.

─── INGREDIENTS ───

Serves 3–4
3 tbsp olive oil
2 shallots, chopped
2 garlic cloves, chopped
1 fresh red chili, chopped
1lb ripe tomatoes, peeled, seeded and
  chopped
1 tbsp tomato paste
1 bay leaf
1 thyme sprig
6 tbsp dry white wine
1lb cooked, peeled large shrimp
salt and black pepper
coarsely torn basil leaves, to garnish

1 Heat the oil in a pan, then add the shallots, garlic and chili and fry until the garlic starts to brown.

2 Add the tomatoes, tomato paste, bay leaf, thyme, wine and seasoning. Bring to a boil, then reduce the heat and cook gently for about 10 minutes, stirring occasionally, until the sauce has thickened. Discard the herbs.

3 Stir the shrimp into the sauce and heat through for a few minutes. Taste and adjust the seasoning. Scatter over the basil leaves and serve at once.

COOK'S TIP
For a milder flavor, remove all the seeds from the chili.

SCALLOPS WITH GINGER

Scallops are at their best at this time of year. Try to find ones with the coral attached, as it is colorful and delicious.

─── INGREDIENTS ───

Serves 4
8–12 shelled scallops
3 tbsp butter
1in piece fresh ginger root,
  finely chopped
1 bunch scallions, diagonally
  sliced
4 tbsp white vermouth
1 cup crème fraîche or heavy cream
salt and black pepper
chopped fresh parsley, to garnish

1 Remove the tough muscle opposite the coral on each scallop. Separate the coral and cut the white part of the scallop in half horizontally.

2 Melt the butter in a frying pan. Add the scallops, including the corals, and sauté for about 2 minutes until lightly browned. Take care not to overcook the scallops as this will toughen them.

3 Lift out the scallops with a slotted spoon and transfer to a warmed serving dish. Keep warm.

4 Add the ginger and scallions to the pan and stir-fry for 2 minutes. Pour in the vermouth and allow to bubble until it has almost evaporated. Stir in the crème fraîche or cream and cook until the sauce has thickened. Taste and adjust the seasoning.

5 Pour the sauce over the scallops, sprinkle with parsley and serve.

SMOKED TROUT PILAF

Smoked trout might seem an unusual partner for rice, but this is a winning combination.

INGREDIENTS

Serves 4

1¼ cups white basmati rice
3 tbsp butter
2 onions, sliced into rings
1 garlic clove, crushed
2 bay leaves
2 whole cloves
2 green cardamom pods
2 cinnamon sticks
1 tsp cumin seeds
4 smoked trout fillets, skinned
½ cup slivered almonds,
   toasted
⅓ cup seedless raisins
2 tbsp chopped fresh parsley
mango chutney and poppadoms,
   to serve

1 Wash the rice thoroughly in several changes of water and drain well. Set aside. Melt the butter in a large frying pan and fry the onions until well browned, stirring frequently.

2 Add the garlic, bay leaves, cloves, cardamom pods, cinnamon and cumin seeds and stir-fry for 1 minute.

3 Stir in the rice, then add 2½ cups boiling water. Bring to a boil. Cover the pan tightly, reduce the heat and cook very gently for 20–25 minutes, until the water has been absorbed and the rice is tender.

4 Flake the smoked trout and add to the pan with the almonds and raisins. Fork through gently. Re-cover the pan and allow the smoked trout to warm in the rice for a few minutes. Scatter over the parsley and serve with mango chutney and poppadoms.

COD WITH SPICED RED LENTILS

INGREDIENTS

Serves 4

1 cup red lentils
¼ tsp ground turmeric
2½ cups fish stock
2 tbsp vegetable oil
1½ tsp cumin seeds
1 tbsp grated fresh ginger root
½ tsp cayenne pepper
1 tbsp lemon juice
2 tbsp chopped fresh coriander
1lb cod fillets, skinned and cut into
*   large chunks*
salt, to taste
coriander leaves and lemon wedges,
*   to garnish*

1 Put the lentils in a pan with the turmeric and stock. Bring to a boil, cover and simmer for 20–25 minutes, until the lentils are just tender. Remove from the heat and add salt.

2 Heat the oil in a small frying pan. Add the cumin seeds and, when they begin to pop, add the ginger and cayenne pepper. Stir-fry the spices for a few seconds, then pour on to the lentils. Add the lemon juice and the coriander and stir in gently.

3 Lay the pieces of cod on top of the lentils, cover the pan and then cook gently over a low heat for about 10–15 minutes, until the fish is tender.

4 Transfer the lentils and cod to warmed serving plates. Sprinkle over the coriander leaves and garnish each serving with one or two lemon wedges. Serve hot.

THAI VEGETABLES WITH NOODLES

This dish makes a delicious vegetarian supper on its own, or serve it as an accompaniment.

INGREDIENTS

Serves 4
8oz egg noodles
1 tbsp sesame oil
3 tbsp groundnut oil
2 garlic cloves, thinly sliced
1in piece fresh ginger root,
*   finely chopped*
2 fresh red chilies, seeded and sliced
4oz broccoli, broken into
*   small florets*
4oz baby corn
6oz shiitake or oyster
*   mushrooms, sliced*
1 bunch scallions, sliced
4oz bok choy or Chinese cabbage,
*   shredded*
4oz bean sprouts
1–2 tbsp dark soy sauce
salt and black pepper

1 Cook the egg noodles in a pan of boiling salted water according to the package instructions. Drain well and toss in the sesame oil. Set aside.

2 Heat the groundnut oil in a wok or large frying pan and stir-fry the garlic and ginger for 1 minute. Add the chilies, broccoli, baby corn and mushrooms and stir-fry for a further 2 minutes.

3 Add the scallions, shredded cabbage and bean sprouts and stir-fry for another 2 minutes.

4 Toss in the drained noodles with the soy sauce and ground black pepper.

5 Continue to cook over a high heat for a further 2–3 minutes, until the ingredients are well mixed and warmed through. Serve at once.

SWISS SOUFFLÉ POTATOES

Economical and satisfying, baked potatoes are great for cold-weather eating. Choose a floury variety of potato for the very best results.

INGREDIENTS

Serves 4
4 medium baking potatoes
4oz Gruyère cheese, grated
½ cup herb-flavored butter
4 tbsp heavy cream
2 eggs, separated
salt and black pepper

1 Preheat the oven to 425°F. Scrub the potatoes, then prick them all over with a fork. Bake for 1–1½ hours until tender. Remove the potatoes from the oven and then reduce the temperature to 350°F.

2 Cut each potato in half and scoop out the flesh into a bowl. Return the potato shells to the oven to crisp them up while making the filling.

3 Mash the potato flesh using a fork, then add the Gruyère, herb-flavored butter, cream, egg yolks and seasoning. Beat well until smooth.

4 Whisk the egg whites in a separate bowl until they hold stiff peaks, then fold into the potato mixture.

5 Pile the mixture back into the potato shells and bake for 20–25 minutes, until risen and golden brown.

NUT PATTIES WITH MANGO RELISH

These spicy patties can be made in advance, if you like, and reheated just before serving.

INGREDIENTS

Serves 4–6
1½ cups finely chopped roasted
   and salted cashew nuts
1½ cups finely chopped
   walnuts
1 small onion, finely chopped
1 garlic clove, crushed
1 green chili, seeded and chopped
1 tsp ground cumin
2 tsp ground coriander
2 carrots, coarsely grated
1 cup fresh white bread crumbs
2 tbsp chopped fresh coriander
1 tbsp lemon juice
1–2 eggs, beaten
salt and black pepper
coriander sprigs, to garnish

For the relish
1 large ripe mango, cut into small cubes
1 small onion, cut into slivers
1 tsp grated fresh ginger root
pinch of salt
1 tbsp sesame oil
1 tsp black mustard seeds

1 Preheat the oven to 350°F. Mix together the chopped nuts, onion, garlic, chili, spices, carrots, bread crumbs, chopped coriander and seasoning in a bowl.

2 Sprinkle over the lemon juice and add enough of the beaten egg to bind the mixture together. Shape the mixture into 12 balls, then flatten slightly into round patties.

3 Place the patties on a lightly greased baking tray and bake for about 25 minutes, until golden brown.

4 Meanwhile, to make the relish, mix together the mango, onion, fresh ginger root and salt.

5 Heat the oil in a small frying pan and add the mustard seeds. Fry for a few seconds until they pop, then stir into the mango mixture. Serve with the nut patties, garnished with coriander.

Spiced Sweet Potato Turnovers

Serves 4

For the filling
1 sweet potato, about 8oz,
   scrubbed
2 tbsp vegetable oil
2 shallots, finely chopped
2 tsp coriander seeds, crushed
1 tsp ground cumin
1 tsp garam masala
4oz frozen baby peas, cooked
1 tbsp chopped fresh mint
salt and black pepper
mint sprigs, to garnish

For the pastry
1 tbsp olive oil
small egg
⅔ cup strained plain yogurt
½ cup butter, melted
2½ cups flour
¼ tsp baking soda
1 tsp paprika
1 tsp salt
beaten egg, to glaze

1 Cook the sweet potato in boiling salted water for 15–20 minutes, until tender. Drain well and leave to cool. Peel the potato and cut the flesh into ½ in cubes.

2 Heat the oil in a frying pan and cook the shallots until softened. Add the sweet potato and fry until it browns at the edges. Add the spices and fry for a few seconds. Remove from the heat and add the peas, mint and seasoning to taste. Leave to cool.

3 Preheat the oven to 400°F. To make the pastry, whisk the oil and egg in a bowl. Stir in the yogurt, then gradually add the melted butter until thoroughly blended.

4 Sift together the flour, baking soda, paprika and salt into a bowl, then gradually stir into the yogurt mixture to form a soft dough. Knead and roll out the dough on a lightly floured surface, then stamp out rounds using a 4in pastry cutter.

5 Spoon about 2 tsp of the filling on to one side of each round, then fold over and seal the edges. Re-roll the trimmings and stamp out more rounds until the filling is used up.

6 Arrange the turnovers on a greased baking sheet and brush with beaten egg. Bake for about 20 minutes, until crisp and golden brown. Serve hot, garnished with mint sprigs.

CAULIFLOWER WITH THREE CHEESES

The flavor of three cheeses gives a new twist to cauliflower cheese.

INGREDIENTS

Serves 4
4 baby cauliflowers
1 cup light cream
3oz dolcelatte cheese, diced
3oz mozzarella cheese, diced
3 tbsp freshly grated Parmesan
  cheese
freshly grated nutmeg
black pepper
toasted bread crumbs, to garnish

COOK'S TIP
If baby cauliflowers are not available, you could use one large cauliflower. Divide into quarters and then remove the central core.

---

1 Cook the cauliflowers in a large pan of boiling salted water for 8–10 minutes, until just tender.

2 Meanwhile, put the cream into a small pan with the cheeses. Heat gently until the cheeses have melted, stirring occasionally. Season with nutmeg and freshly ground pepper.

3 When the cauliflowers are cooked, drain them thoroughly and place one on each of four warmed plates.

4 Spoon a little of the cheese sauce over each cauliflower and sprinkle each with a few of the toasted bread crumbs. Serve at once.

WINTER VEGETABLE HOT-POT

Use whatever vegetables you have to hand in this richly flavored and substantial one pot meal.

INGREDIENTS

Serves 4
2 onions, sliced
4 carrots, sliced
1 small rutabaga, sliced
2 parsnips, sliced
3 small turnips, sliced
½ celeriac, cut into matchsticks
2 leeks, thinly sliced
1 garlic clove, chopped
1 bay leaf, crumbled
2 tbsp chopped fresh mixed herbs, such
  as parsley and thyme
1¼ cups vegetable stock
1 tbsp flour
1½ lb red-skinned potatoes, scrubbed
  and thinly sliced
4 tbsp butter
salt and black pepper

1 Preheat the oven to 375°F. Arrange all the vegetables, except the potatoes, in layers in a large casserole with a tight-fitting lid.

2 Season the vegetable layers lightly with salt and pepper and sprinkle them with garlic, crumbled bay leaf and chopped herbs as you go.

3 Blend the stock into the flour and pour over the vegetables. Arrange the potatoes in overlapping layers on top. Dot with butter and cover tightly.

4 Cook in the oven for 1¼ hours, or until the vegetables are tender. Remove the lid from the casserole and cook for a further 15–20 minutes until the top layer of potatoes is golden and crisp at the edges. Serve hot.

CHOCOLATE CHESTNUT ROULADE

This moist chocolate sponge has a soft, mousse-like texture as it contains no flour. Don't worry if it cracks as you roll it up – this is typical of a good roulade.

INGREDIENTS

Serves 8
6oz semisweet chocolate
2 tbsp strong black coffee
5 eggs, separated
¾ cup sugar
1 cup heavy cream
8oz unsweetened chestnut
   purée
3–4 tbsp confectioners' sugar, plus
   extra for dusting
light cream, to serve

1 Preheat the oven to 350°F. Line a 13 x 9in jelly roll pan with wax paper and brush lightly with oil.

2 Break up the chocolate into a bowl and set over a pan of barely simmering water. Allow the chocolate to melt very gradually, then stir until smooth. Remove the bowl from the pan and stir in the black coffee. Leave the mixture to cool slightly.

3 Whisk the egg yolks and sugar together in a separate, clean bowl, until thick and light, then gently stir in the cooled chocolate and coffee mixture until well combined.

4 Whisk the egg whites in another bowl until they hold stiff peaks. Stir a spoonful into the chocolate mixture to lighten it, then gently fold in the rest.

5 Pour the mixture into the prepared pan, and gently spread level. Bake for 20 minutes. Remove the roulade from the oven, then cover the cooked roulade with a clean dish towel and leave to cool in the pan for several hours, or preferably overnight.

6 Whip the heavy cream until it forms soft peaks. Mix together the chestnut purée and confectioners' sugar until smooth, then fold into the whipped cream.

7 Lay a piece of wax paper on the work surface and dust with confectioners' sugar. Turn out the roulade on to the paper and carefully peel off the lining paper. Trim the sides.

8 Gently spread the chestnut cream evenly over the roulade to within 1in of the edges.

9 Using the wax paper to help you, carefully roll up the roulade as tightly and evenly as possible.

10 Chill the roulade for about 2 hours, then sprinkle liberally with confectioners' sugar. Cut into thick slices and serve with a little light cream poured over each slice.

> COOK'S TIP
> Make sure that you whisk the egg yolks and sugar for at least 5 minutes to incorporate as much air as possible.

CLEMENTINES IN CINNAMON CARAMEL

The combination of sweet, yet sharp clementines and caramel sauce with a hint of spice is divine. Served with strained plain yogurt or crème fraîche, this makes a delicious dessert.

───── INGREDIENTS ─────

Serves 4–6

8–12 clementines
1 cup sugar
2 cinnamon sticks
2 tbsp orange-flavored liqueur
¼ cup shelled pistachio nuts

1 Pare the rind from two clementines using a vegetable peeler and cut it into fine strips. Set aside.

2 Peel the clementines, removing all the pith but keeping them intact. Put the fruits in a serving bowl.

3 Gently heat the sugar in a pan until it dissolves and turns a rich golden brown. Immediately turn off the heat.

4 Cover your hand with a dish towel and pour in 1¼ cups warm water (the mixture will bubble and splutter). Bring slowly to a boil, stirring until the caramel has dissolved. Add the shredded peel and cinnamon sticks, then simmer for 5 minutes. Stir in the orange-flavored liqueur.

5 Leave the syrup to cool for about 10 minutes, then pour over the clementines. Cover the bowl and chill for several hours or overnight.

6 Blanch the pistachio nuts in boiling water. Drain, cool and remove the dark outer skins. Scatter over the clementines and serve at once.

HOT BANANAS WITH RUM AND RAISINS

Choose almost-ripe bananas with evenly colored skins, either all yellow or just green at the tips. Black patches indicate that the fruit is over-ripe.

INGREDIENTS

Serves 4

¼ *cup seedless raisins*

5 *tbsp dark rum*

4 *tbsp unsalted butter*

4 *tbsp light brown sugar*

4 *ripe bananas, peeled and halved*
   lengthwise

¼ *tsp grated nutmeg*

¼ *tsp ground cinnamon*

2 *tbsp slivered almonds, toasted*

chilled cream or vanilla ice cream,
   to serve (optional)

1 Put the raisins in a bowl with the rum. Leave them to soak for about 30 minutes to plump up.

2 Melt the butter in a frying pan, add the sugar and stir until dissolved. Add the bananas and cook for a few minutes until tender.

3 Sprinkle the spices over the bananas, then pour over the rum and raisins. Carefully set alight using a long taper and stir gently to mix.

4 Scatter over the slivered almonds and serve immediately with chilled cream or vanilla ice cream, if you like.

BANANA AND PASSIONFRUIT WHIP

This very easy and quickly prepared dessert is delicious served with crisp cookies.

INGREDIENTS

Serves 4
2 ripe bananas
2 passionfruit
6 tbsp sour cream
⅔ cup heavy cream
2 tsp honey
shortcake or ginger cookies, to serve

1 Peel the bananas, then mash them in a bowl to a smooth purée.

2 Halve the passionfruit and scoop out the pulp. Mix with the bananas and sour cream. Whip the cream with the honey until it forms soft peaks.

3 Carefully fold the cream and honey mixture into the fruit mixture. Spoon into four glass dishes and serve at once with the cookies.

COFFEE JELLIES WITH AMARETTI CREAM

This impressive dessert is very easy to prepare. For the best results, use a high-roasted Arabica bean, preferably from a gourmet coffee shop. Grind the beans until filter-fine, then use to make hot strong coffee.

INGREDIENTS

Serves 4
6 tbsp sugar
1⅛ cups hot strong coffee
2–3 tbsp dark rum or coffee liqueur
4 tsp powdered gelatin

For the coffee amaretti cream
⅔ cup heavy or whipping cream
1 tbsp confectioners' sugar, sifted
2–3 tsp instant coffee granules dissolved in 1 tbsp hot water
6 large amaretti cookies, crushed

1 Put the sugar in a pan with 5 tbsp water and stir over a gentle heat until dissolved. Increase the heat and allow the syrup to boil steadily, without stirring, for 3–4 minutes.

2 Stir the hot coffee and rum or coffee liqueur into the syrup. Sprinkle the gelatin over the top and stir until it is completely dissolved.

3 Pour the jelly mixture into four rinsed-out ⅔ cup molds, allow to cool and then leave in the fridge for several hours until set.

4 To make the amaretti cream, lightly whip the cream with the confectioners' sugar until it holds stiff peaks. Stir in the coffee, then gently fold in all but 2 tbsp of the crushed amaretti cookies.

5 Unmold the jellies on to four individual serving plates and spoon a little of the coffee amaretti cream to one side. Dust over the reserved amaretti crumbs and serve at once.

COOK'S TIP
To ensure that the jellies are crystal-clear, filter the coffee grounds through a paper filter.

CHOCOLATE DATE TORTE

A stunning cake that tastes wonderful. Rich and gooey – it's a chocaholic's delight!

───── INGREDIENTS ─────

Serves 8

scant 1 cup sour cream
scant 1 cup mascarpone
confectioners' sugar, to taste
4 egg whites
½ cup sugar
7oz semisweet chocolate
scant 1 cup Medjool dates, pitted
   and chopped
1½ cups walnuts or pecans,
   chopped
1 tsp vanilla extract, plus a few extra
   drops

1 Preheat the oven to 350°F. Grease and line the base of an 8in spring-form cake pan.

2 To make the frosting, mix together the sour cream and mascarpone, add a few drops of vanilla extract and confectioners' sugar to taste, then set aside.

3 Whisk the egg whites in a bowl until they form stiff peaks. Whisk in 30ml/2 tbsp of the caster sugar until the meringue is thick and glossy, then fold in the remainder.

4 Chop 6oz of the chocolate. Carefully fold into the meringue with the dates, nuts and 1 tsp of the vanilla extract. Pour into the prepared pan, spread level and bake for about 45 minutes, until risen around the edges.

5 Allow to cool in the pan for about 10 minutes, then turn out on to a wire rack. Peel off the lining paper and leave until completely cold. Swirl the frosting over the top of the torte.

6 Melt the remaining chocolate in a bowl over hot water. Spoon into a small paper icing bag, snip off the top and drizzle the chocolate over the torte. Chill before serving, cut in wedges.

WARM LEMON AND SYRUP CAKE

Serves 8
3 eggs
¾ cup butter, softened
¾ cup sugar
1½ cups self-rising flour
½ cup ground almonds
¼ tsp freshly grated nutmeg
2oz candied lemon peel,
* finely chopped*
grated rind of 1 lemon
2 tbsp lemon juice
poached pears, to serve

For the syrup
¾ cup sugar
juice of 3 lemons

1 Preheat the oven to 350°F. Grease and line the base of a deep, round 8in cake pan.

2 Place all the cake ingredients in a large bowl and beat well for 2–3 minutes, until light and fluffy.

3 Tip the mixture into the prepared pan, spread level and bake for 1 hour, or until golden and firm to the touch.

4 Meanwhile, make the syrup. Put the sugar, lemon juice and 5 tbsp water in a pan. Heat gently, stirring until the sugar has dissolved, then boil, without stirring, for 1–2 minutes.

5 Turn out the cake on to a plate with a rim. Prick the surface of the cake all over with a fork, then pour over the hot syrup. Leave to soak for about 30 minutes. Serve the cake warm with thin wedges of poached pears.

TANGERINE YOGURT ICE

Tangerines make a wonderful creamy yogurt ice with a distinctive tangy flavor. Serve scoops in pretty biscuit cups for a special dinner party.

— INGREDIENTS —

Serves 4–6
1lb strained plain yogurt
⅔ cup heavy cream
½ cup sugar
finely grated rind and juice of
  3 tangerines
crisp cookies, to serve

COOK'S TIP
If tangerines aren't available, use clementines, or oranges instead.

1 Put the yogurt, cream and sugar into a bowl. Stir to dissolve the sugar, then add the tangerine rind and juice and mix thoroughly.

2 Pour the mixture into a freezerproof container and freeze until mushy around the edges.

3 Tip the mixture into a food processor and process until the mixture is smooth. Return to the freezer, cover and freeze until firm.

4 To serve, scoop the tangerine yogurt ice into pretty, chilled glasses.

PAPAYA AND PINEAPPLE CRUMBLE

Crumbles are always popular, but you can add excitement with this exotic variation.

— INGREDIENTS —

Serves 4–6
For the topping
1½ cups flour
6 tbsp butter, diced
6 tbsp sugar
¾ cup mixed chopped nuts

For the filling
1 medium ripe pineapple
1 large ripe papaya
1 tbsp sugar
1 tsp cinnamon
grated rind of 1 lime
plain yogurt, to serve

1 Preheat the oven to 350°F. To make the topping, sift the flour into a bowl and rub in the butter until the mixture resembles crumbs. Stir in the sugar and nuts.

2 Peel the pineapple, remove the eyes, then cut in half. Cut away the core and cut the flesh into bite-sized chunks. Halve the papaya and scoop out the seeds using a spoon. Peel, then cut the flesh into similar sized pieces.

3 Put the pineapple and papaya into a large pie dish. Sprinkle over the sugar, cinnamon and lime rind and toss gently to mix.

4 Spoon the crumble topping over the fruit and spread out evenly with a fork, but don't press it down. Bake in the oven for 45–50 minutes, until golden brown. Serve the crumble hot or warm with plain yogurt.

COOK'S TIP
You may need to add a little more sugar to the fruit – especially if the pineapple is quite tart.

INDEX

Apple soufflé omelette, 119
Apricots: apricots in Marsala, 76
  spiced lamb with apricots, 90
Asparagus: asparagus and ham gratin
  16
  asparagus with tarragon butter, 10
Avocados: duck, avocado and
  raspberry salad, 58

Bananas: banana and passionfruit
  whip, 154
  hot bananas with rum and
  raisins, 153
Beans: beans with
  mushrooms, 109
  corn and bean tamale pie, 108
  sausage and bean ragoût, 90
Beef: beef paprika with roasted
  peppers, 92
  bresaola, onion and arugula
  salad, 52
  peppered steaks with Madeira, 93
  rich beef casserole, 132
Beet and herring salad, 86
Blackberry brown sugar meringue,
  117
Blueberries: pear and blueberry pie, 118
  strawberry and blueberry tart, 74
Broccoli and Stilton soup, 122
Bulgur wheat: feta tabbouleh in
  radicchio cups, 52

Carrot and coriander soup, 8
Cauliflower with three cheeses, 148
Celeriac fritters with mustard dip, 128
Cheese: asparagus and ham gratin, 16
  broccoli and Stilton soup, 122
  cauliflower with three cheeses, 148
  crab and ricotta tartlets, 50
  feta tabbouleh in radicchio cups, 52
  fruity ricotta creams, 38
  onion and gruyère tart, 110
  hot tomato and mozzarella
  salad, 10
  marinated goat cheese with
  herbs, 48
  pear and Roquefort salad, 110
  pork with mozzarella and sage, 54
  potato cakes with goat
  cheese, 113
  twice-baked cheddar soufflés, 72
Cherries jubilee, 76
Chicken: chicken baked in a salt
  crust, 94
  chicken parcels with herb
  butter, 23
  chicken, leek and parsley pie, 136
  golden Parmesan chicken, 57
Chicken livers: chicken liver pâté
  with Marsala, 124
  pasta with chicken livers, 94
Chocolate: chocolate amaretti
  peaches, 75
  chocolate chestnut roulade, 150
  chocolate date torte, 156
  hot mocha soufflés, 42
  iced chocolate and nut gâteau, 116

Clementines in cinnamon caramel, 152
Cod: cod baked with tomato sauce, 30
  cod with spiced red lentils, 143
  spicy fish rösti, 26
Coffee: coffee jellies with amaretti
  cream, 154
  hot mocha soufflés, 42
Corn and bean tomale pie, 108
Couscous: root vegetable couscous,
  106
Crab and ricotta tartlets, 50

Dates: chocolate date torte, 156
Duck, avocado and raspberry
  salad, 58

Eggplant: spiced eggplant with
  mint yogurt, 51
Eggs: apple soufflé omelette, 119
  baked eggs with tarragon, 47
  chive omelette stir-fry, 70
  potato and red pepper frittata, 68

Fish: golden fish pie, 105
  Mediterranean fish rolls, 28
  spicy fish rösti, 26
Fruit: fruity ricotta creams, 38
  hot fruit with maple butter, 38
  summer berry medley, 78
  warm autumn compôte, 114

Gooseberry and orange ice cream, 42
Grapefruit: melon and grapefruit
  cocktail, 126

Haddock: seafood crepes, 138
Hake: Spanish-style hake, 104
Herrings: beet and herring
  salad, 86
  herrings with walnut stuffing, 102

Ice cream: brown bread ice cream, 79
  gooseberry and orange ice
  cream, 42
  tangerine yogurt ice, 158

Jerusalem artichoke soup, 122

Lamb: butterflied cumin and garlic
  lamb, 56
  five-spice lamb, 134
  lamb and spring vegetable stew, 20
  oatmeal and herb rack of lamb, 18
  red currant-glazed lamb cutlets, 54
  skewers of lamb with mint, 19
  spiced lamb with apricots, 90
Leeks: chicken, leek and parsley
  pie, 136
  leek terrine with deli meats, 14
  leek, potato and arugula soup, 9
Lemon: warm lemon and syrup
  cake, 157
Lentils: cod with spiced red lentils, 143

Mackerel with mustard and lemon, 24
Mangos: nut patties with mango
  relish, 146

Prosciutto with mango, 126
Melon: melon and grapefruit cocktail, 126
  minted melon salad, 48
Monkfish: monkfish brochettes, 62
  monkfish with Mexican salsa, 101
Mushrooms: beans with
  mushrooms, 109
  mushroom and pancetta pizzas, 88
  spinach roulade with mushrooms,
  34
  trout with mushroom sauce, 102
Mussels: broiled garlic mussels, 129
  tagliatelle with saffron mussels, 100

Nuts: iced chocolate and nut
  gâteau, 116
  nut patties with mango relish, 146

Onions: beet and herring salad, 86
  bresaola, onion and rocket salad, 52
  onion and gruyère tart, 110
  red onion galettes, 69

Papaya and pineapple crumble, 158
Parsnips: spiced parsnip soup, 84
Passionfruit: banana and passion
  fruit whip, 154
Pasta: pasta with chicken livers, 94
  pasta with spring vegetables, 37
  spaghetti with herb sauce, 70
  tagliatelle with saffron mussels,
  100
Peaches: chocolate amaretti
  peaches, 75
Pears: pear and blueberry pie, 118
  pear and Roquefort salad, 110
Peppers: beef paprika with roasted
  peppers, 92
  broiled polenta with peppers, 33
  potato and red pepper frittata, 68
Pheasant: Normandy pheasant, 97
Pineapple: papaya and pineapple
  crumble, 158
Plum and port mousse, 114
Polenta: broiled polenta with
  peppers, 33
Pork: ginger pork with black bean
  sauce, 16
  glazed Chinese-style spare ribs, 58
  pork steaks with gremolata, 133
  pork with mozzarella and sage, 54
Potatoes: creamy potato gratin with
  herbs, 34
  leek, potato and arugula soup, 9
  potato and red pepper frittata, 68
  potato cakes with goat cheese, 113
  Swiss soufflé potatoes, 144
Prosciutto with mango, 126
Pumpkin soup, 85
Raspberries: duck, avocado and
  raspberry salad, 58
  raspberry meringue gâteau, 80
Red snapper with fennel, 61
Rhubarb: rhubarb and ginger
  cheesecake, 40
  rhubarb meringue pie, 41
Rice: smoked trout pilaf, 142

tomato risotto, 32
  wild rice with broiled vegetables, 66
Rock Cornish hens in vermouth, 22

Salad leaves: baby leaf salad with
  croûtons, 66
Salmon: blinis with smoked salmon
  and dill, 89
  salmon rillettes, 125
  salmon with watercress sauce, 29
  sautéed salmon with cucumber, 65
  warm salmon salad, 60
Sausage and bean ragoût, 90
Scallops with ginger, 140
Shrimp: chili shrimp, 140
  garlic shrimp in filo tartlets, 86
  spinach salad with bacon and
  shrimp, 12
Skate with lemon and capers, 98
Sole: sole goujons with lime
  mayonnaise, 26
  sole and pesto parcels, 98
  sole with cider and cream, 30
Spinach: spinach roulade with
  mushrooms, 34
  spinach salad with bacon and
  shrimp, 12
Squash: baked squash with
  Parmesan, 112
Squid: char-broiled squid, 62
Strawberry and blueberry tart, 74
Sweet potatoes: spiced sweet potato
  turnovers, 147

Tangerine yogurt ice, 158
Tomatoes: cod baked with tomato
  sauce, 30
  hot tomato and mozzarella salad, 10
  tomato and basil soup, 46
  tomato risotto, 32
  tuna with pan-fried tomatoes, 64
Trout: smoked trout with cucumber
  salad, 13
  smoked trout pilaf, 142
  trout with mushroom sauce,
  102
Tuna with pan-fried tomatoes, 64
Turkey: stir-fried turkey with
  snow peas, 135

Vegetables: lamb and spring vegetable
  stew, 20
  parcels of baked baby vegetables,
  36
  pasta with spring vegetables, 37
  root vegetable couscous, 106
  Thai vegetables with noodles, 144
  wild rice with broiled vegetables, 66
  winter vegetable hot-pot, 148
Venison: farmhouse venison pie, 96
  venison with cranberry sauce, 130

Whitebait with herb sandwiches, 25